The Grace of Giving

Biblical Expositions

Stephen Olford

Encounter Ministries, Inc.
P. O. Box 757800
Memphis, Tennessee 38175

First printing, August, 1972 – Zondervan Publishing House
Revised edition, November, 1983 – Baker Book House
Second revised edition, December, 1990 – Encounter Ministries, Inc.

Unless otherwise noted, the Scripture quotations used in this publication are from *The New King James Version.* Copyright © 1979, 1980, 1982, Thomas Nelson Inc., Publishers.

ISBN 1-879028-00-X
(previously ISBN 0-8010-6703-0)

Library of Congress Catalog Card Number: 90-08349

Printed by Cushing-Malloy, Inc.
Ann Arbor, Michigan, United States of America

I affectionately dedicate this book
to the members of Calvary Baptist Church
in New York City,
from whom I have learned much concerning
the grace of giving,
and with whom I have had
"fellowship in the gospel."

Contents

Acknowledgments   7

Foreword   9

Introduction   13

1   The Basis of Blessing   21

2   The Essentiality of Giving   29

3   The Example of Giving   37

4   The Ethics of Giving   45

5   The Efficiency of Giving   57

6   The Enrichment of Giving   67

7   The Maintenance of the Ministry   79

Conclusion   91

References   101

Additional Reading   117

Acknowledgments

In commending The Grace of Giving to you I must acknowledge, with gratitude, the advice and assistance I have received from the authors named in these pages, and also the inspiration from the congregation I formerly pastored, to whom this book is dedicated. I also want to thank my dear friend, Dr. Edwin L. (Jack) Frizen, for writing the foreword. Further, I wish to express my warm appreciation to Miss Victoria Kuhl who edited and typed the manuscript, and to Mr. Mark Boorman who assisted in preparing it for publication.

Our efforts will have been exceedingly worthwhile if, through the reading of this book, the God of giving reproduces in us the grace of giving to His eternal glory and the spread of the gospel to the ends of the earth.

Stephen F. Olford

Foreword

It has been said that a man's money, in a mystical sense, is the man himself.

Society applauds the self-made, self-sufficient person. Many are obsessed with getting ahead—the good life, security. Most people regard what they have as theirs by right. They have earned it by their own initiative. They deserve it.

On the other hand, Scripture is full of evidence that all we have comes from God. Man is a created, dependent being and, as such, is a steward of all he has. Man is not the possessor; he is the manager. God created all things; therefore, He owns all things. Man does not possess his own life, time, gifts, wealth. He manages.

One of the most prominent teachings of Scripture is that man is accountable to God. It runs from Genesis through Revelation. Man's inescapable responsibility is that he must someday give account to God (2 Cor. 5:10; Rom. 14:7-12). Self-sufficient or God-dependent, man is a steward whether or not he wants to be.

The clear biblical teaching of this book, *The Grace of Giving*, is critically needed today. Dr. Stephen Olford, one of the most gifted expositors of our time, presents a comprehensive, honest, and deeply perceptive study of financial stewardship.

Dr. Olford carefully notes that the first requisite of stewardship is to give ourselves to God. Logically, the recognition of God's absolute ownership should follow. Our actions should demonstrate the proper management for God of that which He has entrusted to us. Christian stewardship involves doing God's will in all things.

Although Christian stewardship is far broader than the use of finances, giving money is a prominent part of it. Giving is part of worship; it is more important for its spiritual expression than for its financial significance. The stewardship of money is an indication of the reality and depth of commitment to Jesus Christ.

Dr. Olford reveals his pastor's heart in this book. As the son of missionary parents and an international preacher/ evangelist, he has seen the worldwide need for teaching Christian stewardship. As a student and expositor of God's Word, Dr. Olford probes the will of God pertaining to giving that is planned, proportionate, and prayerful. This is true grace giving.

God's Word teaches: (1) giving the first part of income (Deut. 14:23; Prov. 3:9-10), not giving from what is left or if anything is left; (2) giving a tithe (10%) plus other offerings (Mal. 3:8-10); (3) systematic and proportionate giving (1 Cor. 16:2), giving regularly and in proportion to income; and (4) generous and joyful giving (2 Cor. 9:5−13; 8:1-2).

One of the fundamental lessons for Christians is that we cannot outgive God. He is no man's debtor. Henry Parsons Crowell, builder of the great Quaker Oats cereal enterprise, when asked for his average rate of giving, said, "For over forty years I have given sixty to seventy percent of my income to God. But I have never gotten ahead of Him! He has always been ahead of me!"

On a recent flight my seatmate was a San Francisco police captain who was traveling to Chicago for his father's funeral. When he learned that I was a missionary, he mentioned that his father was a minister and had taught him the lifelong practice of tithing. His remark reinforced my conviction that an example of generous and joyful giving should be set in the home.

Financial accountability is a two-way street. The believer is accountable to God for the use of his or her money, and the recipient church or organization is responsible not only before God as to how it is used but also to the Christian public. Full financial disclosure is a must.

One area of stewardship that is often overlooked is in the distribution of property after death. Seven out of eight people die intestate, having made no legal will. It is a tragedy that some who appear to be faithful Christian stewards during their lifetime permit government officials to decide how their final resources will be distributed. Much of it will be absorbed by the state.

We live in an age when even the evangelical Christian church is soft toward disobedience. Scripture says that God will require an accounting for willful disobedience. There is much disobedience—often willful—in the area of giving. Malachi 3:8 asks the question, "Will a man rob God? Yet you have robbed Me! But you say, 'In what way have we robbed You?' In tithes and offerings." No Christian can seriously and sincerely study *The Grace of Giving* and not understand God's standard for financial stewardship. Dr. Olford has demonstrated that the Bible is the Christian's best financial handbook.

Today (1990) there are some five-and-a-half billion people on this planet. Researchers tell us that three-and-a-half billion, including some 12,000 people groups, have not been reached with the gospel of Jesus Christ. We Christians are accountable to God for these souls. Each person must give account for the use of his time, gifts, and wealth. It is a perilous thing to have resources without holding them as a stewardship.

This is a classic book on financial giving. Pastoral staff and lay persons will find it helpful in understanding their responsibilities. It is an excellent guide for church and home Bible studies because it covers a subject on which we need a sound biblical perspective. I am convinced that thorough study and application of the teaching found in *The Grace of Giving* will revolutionize the ministry of many churches. I earnestly commend it to all who seek to do God's will.

Edwin L. Frizen, Jr., D. Miss.
Executive Director
Interdenominational Foreign
Mission Association
Wheaton, Illinois

Introduction

A circus athlete earned his living by displaying astonishing feats of physical strength. His show would normally conclude with a simple, but impressive, demonstration of his ability to squeeze an orange dry! After completing his act, he would then challenge his audience to produce anyone who could extract even one drop of juice from the crushed fruit. On one of these occasions a little man volunteered. He was so diminutive that his very appearance raised a laugh from the spectators. Undaunted, however, the man stepped onto the stage and took from the athlete what appeared to be nothing more than a shriveled up piece of rind. Then bracing himself, he slowly and firmly compressed his right hand. Every eye was on him, and the atmosphere was electric! A moment or two elapsed, and then, to everyone's amazement—and not least the athlete—a drop of orange juice formed and dripped to the floor. As the cheers subsided, the athlete invited the man to come forward, asked his name, and then invited him to tell the crowd how he had managed to develop such fistic powers. "Nothing to it," replied the man, and then added with a grin, "I happen to be the treasurer of the local Baptist church!"

There was a time when I thought that this was a good "offertory" joke; but this is no longer the case. As a pastor and preacher, I have come to see that consecrated and

consistent giving never results from arm-twisting and brow-
beating appeals. Now and again such methods might work,
but in the long run they are doomed to failure.

Perhaps my convictions are best expressed in some
paragraphs that appeared many years ago in what was known
as *The Sunday School Times:*

> Competition for the Christian's dollar among churches,
> religious organizations, and other benevolent groups is
> conducted on a level today that removes giving from the area
> of a spiritual grace. A Wisconsin State College history professor
> made a telling point when he concluded in his study of
> Protestant giving that the doctrine of stewardship has not "had
> much to do with actual human motivation at either the level
> of promotion or the level of giving."
>
> If evangelicals do have a theology of stewardship and giving,
> it is difficult to recognize it in their efforts to raise money—
> efforts which range all the way from a super-pious "this is a
> faith work" to the more crass "I'm doing you a favor to relieve
> you of some of your money." Since believers are bombarded
> with appeals through the mail, from the pulpit, at banquets,
> and over the radio, how can they be expected to arrive at any
> Scriptural view of giving?
>
> The local church and nonchurch related works must bear
> much of the blame for this deplorable state of affairs. If
> believers are not taught a Scriptural doctrine of stewardship,
> can they be expected to give intelligently and can they be
> expected to realize that giving is indeed as vital a spiritual
> ministry as witnessing, reading the Bible, and praying?
>
> If the appeals are based on the techniques of modern
> advertising and selling, will not the response be the same?
> Hence, the glamorous, the emotional, the "squeaking wheel"
> type of promotion gets the best response. Fund raising has
> become a science with "proven" results. Where is the work
> of God the Holy Spirit in this? How does the believer come
> to know the blessed thrill of his gift becoming "an odor of a
> sweet smell, a sacrifice acceptable, wellpleasing unto God"
> (Phil. 4:18)?
>
> On the other hand, Christians must understand that they
> cannot excuse themselves from giving just because much of
> the technique of fund raising does not measure up to Scriptural
> standards. There is no excuse for not giving. But giving must

be in response to the promptings of the Holy Spirit, which may or may not come through an appeal letter or a desperate pulpit or radio plea.

The solution ought never to be one of expedience to achieve the desired goal. If it seems that Christians are not giving as much as they should, this is no reason for financial appeals to degenerate to the methods of modern salesmanship. If a person resents emotional, long-winded appeals this is no reason for him not to give. Asker and giver ought to be motivated by that which is completely in harmony with the example of Scripture. The Apostle Paul was not embarrassed to write of his needs. He reminded the churches of their duty to give, but he never resorted to begging....He taught that giving was indeed a spiritual sacrifice that brought fruit to the account of those who gave.[1]

In common with the author of this editorial, I discovered from the study of the New Testament that the divine concept of giving is a grace; hence the title of this book—*The Grace of Giving*. As you read these pages you will observe a threefold treatment of our subject.

The Basis of Giving

This is dealt with in the first chapter and is based on Malachi 3:7-15. The fact that the basis of giving is found in the Old Testament must not turn you off! Remember that the New Testament is in the Old Testament concealed, and the Old Testament is in the New Testament revealed! The Bible, which includes both Old and New Testaments, is the Word of God. The burden of Malachi 3:7-15 is tithing, which is more than just an Old Testament practice.

Tom Rees, in his book *Money Talks*, reminds us that:

> The early church according to Origen, Jerome and Chrysostom, following the example and teaching of our Lord and the Apostles, both taught and practiced tithing.
>
> Students of Church History tell us that tithing has been practiced widely in the Christian Church since New Testament days.

---

1. *The Sunday School Times*, 1962, p. 455.

Tithes were recognized legally in England as early as A.D. 786, and tithing was a common practice during the reigns of Alfred, Edgar, and Canute.

The Council of Trent (1545) not only enjoined payment of tithes but went so far as to excommunicate those who withheld them!

The principle of tithing is timeless. It is for every man in every age and dispensation. It was neither instituted by the dispensation of law nor terminated by the dispensation of grace. It was neither given by Moses nor abrogated by Jesus Christ.

Tithing was both incorporated into the Law of Moses and into the New Testament Church.

The principle of the Sabbath is similar to that of tithing.

The Sabbath was given by God and practiced by man from the Creation. In every age God has demanded one-seventh of man's time. This timeless principle was not first given with the Law of Moses. It was, however, incorporated into that Law. The wording of the fourth commandment reminds us of this: "Remember the Sabbath day, to keep it holy" (Exod. 20:8). Later, this same principle of one day in seven was by common consent adopted by the New Testament church.

The Lord's day and the Lord's tithe stand or fall together. The New Testament assumes that all enlightened and obedient Christians will both set aside at least one-seventh of their time and one-tenth of their income for the Lord.

Yes, thank God, we "are not under the law, but under grace" (Rom. 6:14); therefore the giving of our money and time is no longer a matter of legality and bondage; but rather of privilege and joyful experience.

If the Hebrews, compelled by Law, gave one-tenth, how can we, constrained by Grace, give one mite less? "What then? Shall we sin, because we are not under the law, but under grace? God forbid....Love is the fulfilling of the law?" (Rom. 6:15; 13:10).[2]

The Barriers to Giving

Here I am reminded of the opening words of an article by Dr. J. C. Macaulay titled "Men Ought to Give." In his characteristic style he writes:

---

2. Tom Rees, *Money Talks,* Hildenborough Hall (Otford Hills, Sevenoaks, Kent, England), p. 33.

The preacher's sermon, according to established custom, had three points: 1) Make all you can; 2) Save all you can; and 3) Give all you can. The senior elder who assumed the prerogative of evaluating the minister's sermons remarked, "Those first two points were grand, but the third spoiled it all."[3]

After fifty years in the ministry I have likewise encountered people who have "hang-ups" when it comes to this matter of giving to God; but I have also discovered that this is nothing new! The Corinthian church experienced the same "hang-ups," and Paul had to deal with them one by one. This explains why I have concentrated on the Corinthian letters in this book. In a positive way I have sought to remove the barriers to giving by spelling out the essentiality, the example, the ethics, and the efficiency of giving. With the appropriate passages before you, examine carefully the unfolding of Paul's doctrine of the grace of giving, and then let the Holy Spirit impart the same grace in you.

The Blessing of Giving

Christians have no conception of what they are missing, in terms of enjoyment and enrichment, until they have learned to give on God's terms. After all, the Lord Jesus said, "It is more blessed to give than to receive" (Acts 20:35). The New English Bible renders these words with even more emphasis: "Happiness lies more in giving than in receiving." No wonder these words of the Lord Jesus have been called "The Supreme Beatitude!" As Tom Rees expressed it:

> The only way to prove the truth of this Beatitude is to put it to the test, and we shall sooner discover from experience that the word of the Master is true—miserly people are miserable people, and generous people are joyous people.[4]

Chapter 7 deals with "The Maintenance of the Ministry." Preachers rarely speak on this subject lest they be accused of seeking raises! But quite seriously, this issue of support for the servants of God is so important that it may well determine the continuance or collapse of missionary work abroad and

3. *I.B.I. News,* London Bible Institute (London, Ont.: Canada), p. 4.
4. Tom Rees, *Money Talks,* p. 9.

evangelistic endeavors at home. I know of missionaries who have had to be recalled from the field. I also know of colleagues in the ministry who have had to exchange the pulpit or platform for the business office to survive financially. "Brethren, these things ought not to be so" (James 3:10). God give us grace to take to heart what is meant by "the maintenance of the ministry." Only sacrificial giving will make possible the battle for souls in a world that is defiled by sin and beguiled by Satan. And when I speak of sacrificial giving I mean giving that is measured and motivated by the cross of Christ. It is nothing less than giving at its best.

Perhaps a story from the past will illustrate what I mean. Early in the nineteenth century the king of Prussia, Frederick William III, found himself in great trouble. He was carrying on expensive wars; he was endeavoring to strengthen his country and make a great nation of the Prussian people. But he did not have enough money to accomplish his plans. He could not disappoint his people, and to capitulate to the enemy would be unthinkable.

After careful reflection he decided to approach the women of Prussia and asked them to bring their gold and silver jewelry to be melted down and made into money for their country. He resolved, moreover, that for each gold or silver ornament he would give in exchange a bronze or iron decoration as a token of his gratitude. Each decoration would bear the inscription, "I gave gold for iron, 1813."

The response was overwhelming. And what was even more important was that these women prized their gifts from the king more highly than their former possessions. The reason, of course, is clear. The decorations were proof that they had sacrificed for their king. Indeed, it is a matter of history that it became unfashionable for women to wear jewelry. So the Order of the Iron Cross was established. Members of this order wore no ornaments, save a cross of iron for all to see.

The church today needs an army of people who are so committed to the King of Kings that sacrifice becomes a way of life! Such an army would do exploits for God. Such an army would hasten the coming and reign of "the King eternal, immortal, invisible, [the] God who alone is wise" (1 Tim.

1:17). Recruits for this army should be known as members of The Order of the Cross of Christ because they have experienced the grace of giving.

1

The Basis
of Blessing

Yet from the days of your fathers you have gone away from My ordinances and have not kept them. Return to Me, and I will return to you, says the Lord of hosts. But you said, In what way shall we return?

Will a man rob God? Yet you have robbed Me! But you say, In what way have we robbed You? In tithes and offerings. You are cursed with a curse, for you have robbed Me, even this whole nation.

Bring all the tithes into the storehouse, that there may be food in My house, and prove Me now in this, says the Lord of hosts, if I will not open for you the windows of heaven and pour out for you such blessing that there will not be room enough to receive it.

And I will rebuke the devourer for your sakes, so that he will not destroy the fruit of your ground, nor shall the vine fail to bear fruit for you in the field, says the Lord of hosts; and all nations will call you blessed, for you will be a delightful land, says the Lord of hosts.

Your words have been harsh against Me, says the Lord, yet you say, What have we spoken against You? You have said, It is vain to serve God; what profit is it that we have kept His ordinance, and that we have walked as mourners before the Lord of hosts? So now we call the proud blessed, for those who do wickedness are raised up; yes, those who tempt God go free.

Malachi 3:7-15

Malachi was the last of the prophets. The times in which he lived—about four hundred years before Christ—were remarkably typical of our day and generation. The religious leaders were failing to proclaim and maintain the laws of God. The house of the Lord was being robbed of its glory and its tithes and offerings. God's chosen people were intermarrying with the pagan nations around them and failing, therefore, to fulfill their rightful responsibilities. So Malachi's message was one of exposure, rebuke, and challenge. Right at the heart of his prophecy, however, this faithful preacher lays down a basis of blessing which applies to all time. In Malachi's day, the blessing was primarily material and physical; but in this church age God's purpose for His people is also that of spiritual refreshment, a delight in the presence of the Lord. Look, then, at these conditions and observe that if "the windows of heaven" are to be opened to us in fullness of blessing there must be:

A Moral Restoration

"'Yet from the days of your fathers you have gone away from My ordinances and have not kept them. Return to Me, and I will return to you,' says the Lord of hosts." In the philosophy of divine blessing there is no substitute for repentance and obedience. When nations or individuals depart from the laws of God and manifest a spirit of rebellion, heaven demands nothing less than moral restoration. This means:

A Restoration Which Is Initiated by Repentance

Return to Me, and I will return to you, says the Lord of hosts.

Repentance signifies a change of mind leading to a change of heart and life. In essence, it is a complete turnaround, a coming back with deep contrition and humility to an offended and grieved God. Remember that sin is not only a departure from righteousness, but a departure from God Himself.

Therefore, repentance is nothing less than a return to God Himself. And the wonder of it all is that when we return He returns also. "Return to Me," He says, "and I will return to you." In New Testament language, John puts it this way: "If we confess our sins, He is faithful and just to forgive us our sins and to cleanse us from all unrighteousness" (1 John 1:9). If we do not know the fullness of blessing in our lives, then it is because we have wandered from God. We are in a far-off place, and God is saying to us "Return."

But there is something more than repentance here.

A Restoration Which is Perpetuated by Obedience

Yet from the days of your fathers you have gone away from My ordinances and have not kept them.

God has linked blessing to a life of obedience—"Do this and you will live" (Luke 10:28). This is not just a piece of legalism, it is a divine principle of life and blessing. Malachi solemnly reminds his people that they had departed from God's ordinances, even as their fathers before them. Through Samuel this favored nation had learned and known that "to obey is better than sacrifice, and to heed than the fat of rams" (1 Sam. 15:22); therefore, there was no excuse.

If we want "the windows of heaven" to be opened upon our lives we must fulfill these conditions of repentance and obedience. This is the only way of moral restoration.

The second condition laid down in our text is:

A Material Restitution

"Bring all the tithes into the storehouse." The principle of material giving to God is consistent and absolute throughout Holy Scripture. When we give, God blesses; and, conversely, when we withhold God curses. So God says, "You are cursed with a curse, for you have robbed Me, even this whole nation."

Malachi had to challenge the nation to "bring...the tithes" because his people had failed to do this. This is why they were not living in blessing. This word on material restitution is not addressed to givers but to withholders.

The Place of This Restitution

Bring all the tithes into the storehouse.

From the time of Hezekiah (2 Chron. 31:11) there was in the sanctuary a storehouse built for depositing the tithes and offerings of the people. This was also true of the second temple in the days of Nehemiah (Neh. 10:38, 39). But even before this God clearly states that all the tithes and offerings of the people were to be brought to one place. In fact, if a man lived too far away to carry his corn, wine or firstlings of his herds and flocks, he was instructed to turn his goods into money in order that he might "go to the place which the Lord [his] God chooses" (Deut. 14:22-29).

The New Testament counterpart of this principle is the giving of all tithes by the members to the local church. The disbursements of money may and should include needs beyond the local church, but the responsibility to bring *all* the tithes to the local church is illustrated in the Old Testament and indicated in the New Testament. One of the great sins of our time is the robbing and defrauding of the local church by its membership. Until such restitution is made God will not bless. This is what is meant by "storehouse tithing"— bringing our tithes to the place where our membership is established, our spiritual life is nourished, and our church privileges are enjoyed. If we give elsewhere, then it should be over and above the required tithe to our church. This is scripturally binding upon all who desire to see the blessing of God.

The Proportion of This Restitution

Bring all the tithes into the storehouse.

Tithing is four hundred years older than the law. Abraham gave tithes to God through Melchizedek, the king-priest (Gen. 14:17; 15:1). According to the seventh chapter of Hebrews, Melchizedek is a beautiful type of Christ in resurrection. Melchizedek gives Abraham bread and wine, symbols of service; and Abraham acknowledges his indebtedness to God by giving Him tithes of all his spoils. In other words, tithing is the scriptural way of saying thank you to God for all that

He has done for us.

In his book *Giving to God,* Robert A. Laidlaw illustrates this thought: "I go to a home where there is a little girl, five or six years of age, and give her a box of chocolates. She straightway disappears, and when she returns her lips and fingers are covered with chocolate. In another home, however, the box is opened at once, and the little lassie brings it to me and says, 'You have the first one.' 'Oh, no!' I say, 'they are for you.' 'But please,' she pleads, 'you brought them to me. Do please have the first one.' And helping myself I say, 'Thank you, dear.' Which child has the warmest place in my affections, and which is more likely to get another box of chocolates?" So the tithe is the first chocolate handed back to God. For some, it will be one-tenth of the total income (as the word indicates); for others, it will be more. Never will it be less.

Then there are the offerings. This word means the "freewill giving," which is over and above the basic tithe. The Bible teaches that God demands the tithes, whereas He deserves our offerings. He demands the tithes because such giving is for our good and blessing. He deserves the offering, for such overflow from our hearts satisfies His heart.

One Sunday morning a pastor told his small congregation that the church faced an urgent need for a $1,000 missionary offering. He did not pressure his parishioners, but merely said that if they would give cheerfully as the Lord directed the need would be met. A six-year old boy was so impressed with the pastor's words that he spoke to his mother. "I feel God wants me to give $100." His mother was surprised...that amount seemed far too much for a young boy to give. Besides, she had already decided to make a sacrificial contribution herself. When she saw the seriousness of the child, she stood to her feet and asked the pastor if she could speak to the congregation. As she announced her son's intention, the congregation was electrified. The boy's father quickly offered to provide the $100, but the youngster shook his head. "I've saved that much money, and I want to give it to the missionaries so that others can know Jesus." His words convicted many hearts; wallets and purses were reopened. When the offering was received the goal of $1,000 was easily surpassed. Openhearted financial support of the church and its missionary outreach honors the Lord.[1]

Notice that giving is older than the law (Gen. 14:17; 15:1), was enforced by the law (Lev. 27:30-33), was approved by our Lord (Matt. 23:23), and was included in the teaching of the apostles (1 Cor. 16:2).

Have we been robbing God? Then this is the proportion of restitution which He expects of us if "the windows of heaven" are to be opened on our lives.

The Purpose of This Restitution

Bring all the tithes into the storehouse, that there may be food in My house.

The tithes and offerings were the only means by which the priests lived; they had no inheritance of their own (Num. 18:20-32). In a similar way, God has ordained that the church should function by means of the tithes and offerings of His believing people (1 Cor. 9:1-14). What is more, the general teaching of the New Testament makes it evident that in normal circumstances each local assembly should be self-supporting.

With this purpose in view, God "curses" those who rob Him. To hold back what is His due in a local church is to merit the judgment of God. This happened in the early history of Israel in Canaan, and it also happened in the early history of the church. Achan's sin was robbing God of the gold of Jericho, which was dedicated and designated for the Lord's treasury (Josh. 6:18-19). The penalty was death. What was true of this individual eventually became true of the whole nation, in Malachi's day, so that God had to say, "You have robbed Me." The sin of Ananias and Sapphira was that of robbing God and the penalty was death (Acts 5). The church age ends with the same problem when the risen Lord says to a niggardly Christendom, "You are wretched, miserable, poor, blind, and naked" (Rev. 3:14-22).

Failure to give is equivalent to thievery, and God insists that until there is a moral restoration and a material restitution

---

1. *Our Daily Bread.* Copyright © 1981 by Radio Bible Class, Grand Rapids, Michigan 49555 [September 6].

there will be no fullness of blessing. Give heed, then, to the place, proportion, and purpose of this material restitution.

If such conditions are faithfully met, there is what our text describes as the opened "windows of heaven" or what we might call:

A Miraculous Realization

"'Prove Me now in this,' says the Lord of hosts, 'if I will not open for you the windows of heaven.'" What a concept this is of God's lavish blessing—"windows of heaven." This is revival—the outpouring of the Spirit for which we all should seek. We cannot work it up, for it is the miraculous realization of God's presence and power. It is the proving of God in personal experience. Consider what this blessing includes:

The Rewarding of Our Faith

I will...open for you the windows of heaven and pour out for you such blessing that there will not be room enough to receive it.

What was to be a physical fulfillment of Deuteronomy 11:13-15 in Israel's day is intended to be a spiritual fulfillment in our day. God waits to visit us with "times of refreshing" (Acts 3:19) and flood tides of abundance. The original Hebrew language describing the extent of God's blessing is difficult to translate. Literally, it means "until there is sufficiency" which, of course, is understood to signify "until there is no more need." In such a fulfillment faith is more than rewarded. Oh, for such a revival!

The Rebuking of Our Foes

I will rebuke the devourer for your sakes.

The locusts had eaten the crops, and the mildew and blasting had destroyed what was left. These physical pests and destroying elements represented the enemies of the people of God. Today they symbolize the forces of Satan that are arrayed against the church. Outside of the experience of revival there is no authority to rebuke the devil and his hordes, but once God breaks through from heaven the enemy is rendered helpless and hopeless. This is what Isaiah means when he says, "When the enemy comes in like a flood, the Spirit of the Lord will lift up a standard against him" (Isa. 59:19).

In *The Abbot,* Sir Walter Scott wrote, "There is a popular belief respecting evil spirits, that they cannot enter an uninhabited house unless invited, nay dragged over the threshold." If our hearts are occupied completely by the Spirit of the living God, the powers of Satan are already defeated.

The Renewing of Our Fruitfulness

And all nations will call you blessed, for you will be a delightful land, says the Lord of hosts.

Malachi is saying that when the surrounding nations see the prosperity which follows true giving to God, they will rightly judge that it is the Lord's action in blessing the people.

The world is generally unimpressed by the church's witness today. The average person considers it irrelevant; the businessman regards it as pathetically inefficient, while the journalist maintains that religious news is little or no news! But what would happen if the floodgates of heaven were opened and revival blessings were poured out on our local congregations and the church at large? Multitudes would throng our buildings, the businessman would take notice, and the reporter would write headlines in the press. The nations would call us blessed.

God's purpose for the church is that she should be "a delightful land"—a paradise of fruitfulness and fragrance. Since the church is made up of individuals it comes down to you and me. Is "the fruit of the Spirit" evident in our lives? Are we living in revival? Is our witness making an impact on contemporary society? If not, then let us face seriously and urgently ponder the true basis of blessing.

2

The Essentiality of Giving

Behold, I tell you a mystery: We shall not all sleep, but we shall all be changed—in a moment, in the twinkling of an eye, at the last trumpet. For the trumpet will sound, and the dead will be raised incorruptible, and we shall be changed. For this corruptible must put on incorruption, and this mortal must put on immortality. So when this corruptible has put on incorruption, and this mortal has put on immortality, then shall be brought to pass the saying that is written: Death is swallowed up in victory.

O Death, where is your sting? O Hades, where is your victory? The sting of death is sin, and the strength of sin is the law. But thanks be to God, who gives us the victory through our Lord Jesus Christ.

Therefore, my beloved brethren, be steadfast, immovable, always abounding in the work of the Lord, knowing that your labor is not in vain in the Lord.

Now concerning the collection for the saints, as I have given orders to the churches of Galatia, so you must do also: on the first day of the week let each one of you lay something aside, storing up as [God] may prosper, that there be no collections when I come.

And when I come, whomever you approve by your letters, I will send to bear your gift to Jerusalem. But if it is fitting that I go also, they will go with me.

1 Corinthians 15:51 — 16:4

The First Epistle to the Corinthians begins with the affirmation that "God is faithful, by whom [we are] called into the fellowship of His Son, Jesus Christ our Lord" (1 Cor. 1:9). This theme is then developed with accompanying words of correction and instruction to show that there pulsates throughout the whole church of Christ one common resurrection life by the indwelling presence of the Holy Spirit. The letter finally concludes with the words, "Therefore, my beloved brethren, be steadfast, immovable, always abounding in the work of the Lord, knowing that your labor is not in vain in the Lord. Now concerning the collection for the saints ....On the first day of the week let each one of you lay something aside, storing up as [God] may prosper."

In the original Greek there is no break between what we call the 15th and 16th chapters. So Paul is virtually saying that a shared resurrection life in Christ is a serving life. The Lord Jesus gave Himself in death and resurrection, not in order to save us from sacrifice, but rather to teach us how to give ourselves and our substance in continual sacrifice. Thus Paul finds no difficulty in moving from the theological heights of chapter 15 to the practical depths of chapter 16.

The occasion of this instruction in the grace of giving was a crisis in the church at Jerusalem. Because of persecution and opposition, many believers had suffered the despoiling of their goods and some even the loss of their lives, and Paul felt it was his duty to provide financial assistance for such poverty-stricken saints in the mother church.

Embedded in Paul's admonition are principles that will abide for all time. We do well, therefore, to consider the essentiality of giving in three aspects:

The Purposeful Regularity of Giving to God

"On the first day of the week let each one of you lay something aside, storing up." Orderliness and regularity are two characteristics of our God. We see this in nature as well as in the church. The word to His believing people is, "Let all things be done decently and in order" (1 Cor. 14:40). So in the matter of giving we have definite instruction about the importance of purposeful regularity.

The Establishment of the Habit of Giving

On the first day of the week.

The history of the church reveals that "the first day of the week" quickly became the day of worship, giving, and service for the people of God. Indeed, our text appears to be the earliest mention of this fact. On what better day, therefore, could Christians take time to settle their accounts with God?

In Old Testament times the tithe, generally speaking, was an annual tax; but in the New Testament we find that giving to God was to be a weekly contribution. In God's wise economy this was to be the remedy for our lack of discipline, irregularity, and indifference in our acts of worship. Oh, that God would indelibly impress on us this holy habit of giving on the first day of the week!

Gladis and Gordon DePree get to the heart of the matter of our gifts to God:

> Someone will raise the inevitable questions: Does God lack for anything? Why should I give to Him my limited means, my precious time, my one short life? Will it make Him, owner of a universe, any richer? No. But it will make me, creature of God, more than a dead-end receptacle. It will make me a live being through which life flows back to God.[1]

The Encouragement of the Honor of Giving

On the first day of the week let each one of you lay something aside, storing up...that there be no collections when I come.

All giving to God should be a matter of theological conviction, leading to practical expression. Too often we have dishonored this holy habit by using carnal pressures to extract money from uninstructed and undisciplined Christians.

---

1. Gladis and Gordon DePree, *A Blade of Grass* (Grand Rapids: Zondervan, 1967), p. 15, adapted.

The apostle Paul insists that giving is not only a holy habit but also a high honor. This is why he wanted the collections to be made before his arrival in Corinth. He did not want their generosity to depend upon his presence. How far removed is this from the general practice in churches today! With shame we have to confess that often certain preachers are asked to occupy pulpits because it is known that their presence will ensure a good offering. This is unscriptural and certainly unspiritual.

It is obvious that purposeful regularity of giving to God is bound up with the habit and honor of this ministry. We should never forget this essential principle.

The Personal Responsibility of Giving to God

"Let each one of you lay something aside, storing up." Although these words are addressed to the whole church throughout time they also have a particular relevance for the local assembly. Paul was writing to the church of God which was at Corinth (1 Cor. 1:2). What was true of Corinth could be true of any local congregation today. With this in mind, note two things:

The Inclusiveness of this Personal Responsibility

Let each one of you lay something aside.

No member is excluded. The words are specific and the application is inescapable. Old and young, rich and poor, must all be involved in this matter of Christian giving. As Paul reveals later in his second letter to the Corinthians, the churches of Macedonia gave liberally and did so out of "deep poverty" (2 Cor. 8:2). Our Lord commended the widow's mite to teach us that no one could be too poor to give, but He also received the wealth of Barnabas to demonstrate that no one could be too rich to sacrifice for God!

This principle of personal responsibility goes even deeper. Money has an inclusiveness about it because God always associates the gift with the giver; giving is essentially personal. Money has no value whatsoever, unless it is the expression of life, labor, and love. Furthermore, God has no favorites in His purpose of blessing, and since He wants to bless everyone He expects everyone to give. This is why the Lord Jesus said, "It is more blessed to give than to receive" (Acts 20:35).

On his tenth birthday a sensitive boy received ten shiny silver dollars from a thoughtful uncle. The child was very appreciative. He immediately sat down on the floor and spread the coins before him. Then he began to plan how to use the money. He set aside the first dollar saying, "This one is for Jesus." He then went on to decide what to do with the second, and so on until he came to the last dollar. "This one is for Jesus," he said. The boy's mother interrupted, "But I thought you gave the first dollar to Jesus." "I did," the boy replied. "The first one really belongs to Him, but this one is a gift to Him from me."

A Directive Concerning this Personal Responsibility

Let each one of you lay something aside, storing up.

The thought conveyed in the phrase, "lay something aside, storing up," is quite suggestive. In one translation it reads "form a little hoard." This, of course, is the proper kind of hoarding. It is something which is deliberately and dedicatively set aside for the Lord Himself. It involves thought, time, and planning in this whole matter of giving to God and puts to shame the present-day procedure of so many who come to worship without the preparation or consecration of their gifts. So we see that this laying something aside, this storing up, is an activity of disciplined giving which takes place before the money is brought to the central treasury of the church. This obviates any hastiness or untidiness in the whole area of giving. It is clear, therefore, that all giving represents personal responsibility to God. No one is excluded and no one can act without thoughtfulness or deliberateness.

But there is still another aspect which deserves our investigation.

The Practical Reciprocity of Giving to God

"Lay...aside...as [God] may prosper." Years ago Hudson Taylor, founder of the China Inland Mission, started each new year by writing a check to the order of The Hebrew Christian Testimony to Israel in London. He marked it "to the Jew first." When David Baron, the saintly, scholarly leader of that fine organization, received the gift he immediately reciprocated and sent his own personal gift to the CIM with the notation, "and also to the Greek."[2]

Reciprocity is the principle of taking and giving, and what Paul is teaching here is that we cannot always be taking without giving. If we have any sense of reasonableness and responsiveness, we are bound to reciprocate by giving back in some measure what God lavishes on us.

Two thoughts emerge:

The Consideration of What We Receive of God

Lay something aside...as [God] may prosper.

We must remember that the prospering of God is never limited to the material gains of our daily work. Spiritually, He blesses us "with every spiritual blessing...in Christ" (Eph. 1:3); physically, He prospers us with health and strength, "for in Him we live and move and have our being" (Acts 17:28); temporally, He "daily loads us with benefits" (Ps. 68:19). Over and above this He supplies what we need to live our normal lives: the talents, time, and strength for our toil. These are all His gifts. We need to remember this when we face up to our responsibilities of giving to God. All giving reflects the measure of our appreciation of God's prospering hand upon us.

The Calculation of What We Should Return to God

Lay something aside...as [God] may prosper.

Before we decide on our regular giving it is well to point out that the collection for which Paul was asking was something over and above the normal giving of the church at Corinth. Of the six or more words that are used in the New Testament to describe our monetary gifts to God, the apostle uses a special term in our text which means "an extra

---

2. Daniel Fuchs, "Does God Play Favorites with the Jews?" *The Chosen People,* January 1982:11.

collection." The Greek word *logia* denotes that which was opposite to a tax; in other words, it was extra giving.

Note further that Paul does not state the exact amount that we are to give to God, but leaves the matter open to the practical reasonableness of every yielded believer. Instructed Christians, in the apostle's day, would know that under the law the Jew was bound to give one-tenth of his income to God. Then, of course, there were freewill offerings, trespass offerings, and costly journeys to the temple. It has been estimated that the aggregate of religious gifts among the Jews in olden times could not have been less than one-fifth of each man's income, and some very probably involved one-third of it. This is something to bear in mind when we talk so glibly about a basic tithe.

If the Old Testament saints, under law, could give amounts of this kind, can we, under grace, give God any less? So the New Testament leaves this matter wide open for us to act in proportion to the prospering of God. It is important to emphasize, in this connection, that yielded believers have given everything to God. Were this not so, there would be no basis for Christian giving. But having made that clear, the Bible goes on to show that, in terms of practical living, while everything may be dedicated to God He also demands in cash or equivalent the basic tithe, and still deserves in cash or equivalent the extra offering. For some, giving will represent more than this, but for no one will it involve less.

The final word is summed up in the passage under consideration: "Let each one of you lay something aside, storing up as [God] may prosper." If there is a genuine consideration of what we receive of God, there will be a genuine calculation of what we return to Him. Such giving will cost because the cross inspires it and the church requires it! And this is how heaven has planned it; we must give to keep the work of God alive!

In his book, *The Royal Route to Heaven,* Dr. Alan Redpath cites the following story:

> A certain Christian once said to a friend, "Our church costs too much. They are always asking for money." [Her friend

replied in this fashion]: "Some time ago a little boy was born in our home. He cost [us] a lot of money from the very beginning: he had a big appetite, he needed clothes, medicine, toys, and even a puppy. Then he went to school, and that cost a lot more; later he went to college, then he began dating, and that cost a small fortune! But in his senior year at college he died, and since the funeral he hasn't cost [us] a penny. Now which situation do you think [we] would rather have?" After a significant pause the friend continued, "As long as this church lives it will cost. When it dies for want of support it won't cost us anything. A living church has the most vital message for all the world today, therefore I am going to give and pray with everything I have to keep our church alive."[3]

We have considered the essentiality of giving. Taking this truth seriously will make great demands on us. Before we refuse to bow to the Word of God, let us remember that this is the price of keeping our church alive, and she must live if the Savior is to be glorified and the world is to be evangelized. May God give us the grace, then, to be purposeful, personal, and practical in our giving, and blessing will most surely come to our lives as well as to our church.

---

3. Alan Redpath, *The Royal Route to Heaven* (Westwood, N.J.: Revell, 1960), pp. 226-227. Used by permission.

3

The Example
of Giving

Moreover, brethren, we make known to you the grace of
God bestowed on the churches of Macedonia; that in a great
trial of affliction the abundance of their joy and their deep
poverty abounded in the riches of their liberality.

For I bear witness that according to their ability, yes, and
beyond their ability, they were freely willing, imploring us
with much urgency that we would receive the gift and the
fellowship of the ministering to the saints.

And this they did, not as we had hoped, but first gave
themselves to the Lord, and then to us by the will of God.
So we urged Titus, that as he had begun, so he would also
complete this grace in you as well. But as you abound in
everything — in faith, in speech, in knowledge, in all
diligence, and in your love for us — see that you abound
in this grace also. I speak not by commandment, but I am
testing the sincerity of your love by the diligence of others.

For you know the grace of our Lord Jesus Christ, that
though He was rich, yet for your sakes He became poor,
that you through His poverty might become rich.

2 Corinthians 8:1-9

Paul's conception of giving is a lofty one. To him *giving is
a grace,* a ministry of the Holy Spirit inwrought in personal
experience and outworked in practical expression. Wherever

37

he planted churches the apostle made it his business to instruct the people of God in the doctrine of Christian giving. As a consequence, the churches in Macedonia, such as Thessalonica, Berea, and particularly Philippi, were renowned for their charity and liberality.

In the passage before us, the apostle brings this fact to the attention of the Corinthians and concludes the paragraph with the supreme example of the self-giving of our Lord. Apparently, even though this assembly abounded in such gifts as "faith,...speech,...knowledge, [and] all diligence," *it lacked in the grace of giving.* So Paul confronts them with two examples of giving to produce in them a sense of responsibility in Christian giving. Let us look at these examples and learn the lessons that God would teach us.

The Example of Human Giving

"Moreover, brethren, we make known to you the grace of God bestowed on the churches of Macedonia." The New English Bible makes this clearer by rendering the text as follows: "We must tell you, friends, about the grace of generosity which God has imparted to our congregation in Macedonia." As Paul indicated already in his first letter to the Corinthians, the occasion of this interchurch money-raising program was the need of Jewish Christians in Jerusalem. Persecution and privation had left the mother church in desperate need of assistance. When news of this reached the believers in Macedonia they rose nobly to the challenge. "Now," says Paul, addressing the Corinthians, "you do likewise." Then he proceeds to describe in detail the example of this giving on the part of the Macedonians.

It Was Sacrificial Giving

Moreover, brethren, we make known to you the grace of God bestowed on the churches of Macedonia: that in a great trial of affliction the abundance of their joy and their deep poverty abounded in the riches of their liberality.

Dr. J. H. Jowett has said, "Ministry that costs nothing accomplishes nothing." Paul takes great care to show that it was not in circumstances of prosperity that the saints in Macedonia gave their liberal offering. Some severe test of affliction had come on these local churches (Acts 16:20; 17:5, 13; Phil. 1:28; 1 Thess. 1:6; 2:14; 3:3-9) and they had been reduced to what is described as "deep poverty" or, more literally, "down-to-the-bottom poverty." But in all their affliction and poverty there was joy and liberality. This is true sacrifice, and they had learned it from their matchless Savior, "who for the joy that was set before Him endured the cross, despising the shame" (Heb. 12:2).

Dr. Roy L. Laurin tells of a Christian businessman who was traveling in Korea. In a field by the side of the road was a young man pulling a rude plow while an old man held the handles. The businessman was amused and took a snapshot of the scene. "That is curious! I suppose these people are very poor," he said to the missionary who was interpreter and guide to the party. "Yes," was the quiet reply, "those two men happen to be Christians. When their church was being built, they were eager to give something toward it; but they had no money. So they decided to sell their one and only ox and give the proceeds to the church. This spring they are pulling the plow themselves." The businessman was silent for some moments. Then he said, "That must have been a real sacrifice." "They did not call it that," said the missionary, "they thought themselves fortunate that they had an ox to sell!" When the businessman reached home he took the picture to his pastor and told him all about it. Then he added, "I want to double my giving to the church and do some *plow* work. Up until now I have never given God anything that involved real sacrifice."[1]

The Macedonians gave with joy and liberality. It was sacrificial giving.

It Was Spontaneous Giving

For I bear witness that according to their ability, yes, and

---

1. Adapted from *II Corinthians: Where Life Endures.* Copyright © 1946 by Roy L. Laurin (Findlay, Ohio: Dunham), p. 158.

beyond their ability, they were freely willing, imploring us
with much urgency that we would receive the gift and the
fellowship of the ministering to the saints.

From Scripture it is clear that the grace of giving is not so much the result of outward compulsion as the consequence of inward expulsion! In a very real sense it is "the expulsive power of a new affection." Paul admits that he had no authority to demand offerings from the Corinthian saints, but he could certainly offer them the opportunity to test "the sincerity of [their] love." The example he holds up is that of the giving of these Macedonians who sacrificed even beyond their power. The secret was simple: "they gave of their own free will." This is an accurate rendering of the phrase, "they were freely willing." What is more, they took the initiative in imploring Paul "with much urgency" that he would receive their gifts as a token of their fellowship with the saints in Jerusalem.

Spontaneous giving is not careless giving. Rather, it is giving that is prompted by the Spirit of God and guided by the Word of God. What an example these dear saints of Macedonia are to the church of our day! Would to God that we knew something of sacrifice and spontaneity in our giving!

But there is still another lesson in their example of stewardship:

It Was Spiritual Giving

And this they did, not as we had hoped, but first gave
themselves to the Lord, and then to us by the will of God."

Their giving was the outward expression of their utter dedication to God or, as someone has put it, "The crowning point of their generosity was their complete self-surrender."

There is a kind of giving which is unspiritual; it has ulterior motives. One form of it draws attention to one's self. The Lord Jesus soundly condemned such a motive in His Sermon on the Mount. He said, "When you do a charitable deed, do not let your left hand know what your right hand is doing, that your charitable deed may be in secret" (Matt. 6:3-4). Another form of unspiritual giving is to bring our offerings to God with a spirit of illwill and reluctance. This, of course, runs contrary to the apostolic injunction to give "not grudgingly or of necessity; for God loves a cheerful giver" (2 Cor. 9:7). The worst form of giving, however, is that of attempting to buy off one's indebtedness to God.

How different was the spirit of the Macedonians! Their giving was not ostentatious, but joyous and generous. Moreover, it was accompanied by an act of complete self-surrender. The construction of the verse indicates that the giving of themselves to the Lord and to the apostle was a deeper act of commitment. The word *first* is not used here in a temporal sense, but rather with the idea of the prior claim—"They ...first gave themselves to the Lord, and then to us by the will of God." This means that before they gave generously these people had dedicated themselves afresh to the Lord, placed themselves unreservedly in the apostle's hands for the service of Christ, and then provided the monetary support for the saints in Jerusalem. This is spiritual giving! What an example of human giving! What was their secret? Surely it lies in the manner of their giving as the measure of their love for Christ, their Savior and Lord.

It is said that when the British government sought to reward General Gordon for his brilliant service in China, he declined all money and titles, but accepted a gold medal inscribed with the record of his thirty-three engagements. It was his most prized possession. But after his death the medal could not be found. Eventually it was learned that he had sent it to Manchester during a severe famine, directing that it should be melted down and used to buy food for the poor. In his diary under the date of its sending were these words found written in his diary: "The last earthly thing I had in this world that I valued I have given to the Lord Jesus Christ."

Wonderful as is the example of human giving, Paul does not leave us at this point. He immediately proceeds to describe:

The Example of Divine Giving

"For you know the grace of our Lord Jesus Christ, that though He was rich, yet for your sakes He became poor, that you through His poverty might become rich." In this one all-embracing sentence Paul shows that the Holy Spirit who prompted the Macedonians in their giving is the same eternal Spirit who sustained the Savior when He "offered Himself without spot to God" (Heb. 9:14).

Christ's Giving Was Sacrificial

For you know the grace of our Lord Jesus Christ, that though He was rich, yet for your sakes He became poor.

The tense of the verb suggests that the fact of the incarnation, rather than the conditions under which Jesus lived, was uppermost in Paul's mind. To the apostle, Christ became poor in the very act of becoming man! He was awed by the condescension and sacrifice of our Lord in contracting to the measure of a woman's womb. So he declares in another place: "And without controversy great is the mystery of godliness: God was manifested in the flesh" (1 Tim. 3:16).

Think of Christ as rich in power, yet humbly submitting to human weakness; rich in glory, yet willingly laying aside that effulgence for the likeness of men; rich in wisdom, yet mysteriously surrendering the independent use of His mind in order to become subject to His Father's judgment; rich in resources, yet having no room at His birth (Luke 2:7), no home in His life (Matt. 8:20), and no grave at His death (Matt. 27:59-60).

To Paul, and to those who have sensibilities at all, this is grace; this is unmerited favor; this is unbounded kindness; this is sacrifice in giving at its loftiest and best. Such grace and sacrifice cause us to exclaim:

> Θ matchless grace, that Jesus there alone
> On Calvary's cross, for sinners did atone:
> To such a Friend, our Saviour and our King
> Our lives for service we will gladly bring.
>
> T.L. Hargrave

Christ's Giving Was Spontaneous

Though He was rich, yet for your sakes He became poor.

In perfect harmony with the Father and the Holy Spirit, He

took the initiative in coming to earth to give Himself a ransom for you and me. Paul spells out the spontaneity of self-giving when he writes: "The righteousness of faith speaks in this way, 'Do not say in your heart, "Who will ascend into heaven?" (that is, to bring Christ down from above) or, "Who will descend into the abyss?" (that is, to bring Christ up from the dead)'" (Rom. 10:6-7). Whether it was the condescending grace of the incarnation or the conquering grace of the resurrection, it was all of Christ. This is heaven's standard of giving and there is no substitute for it.

Christ's Giving Was Spiritual

He became poor, that you through His poverty might become rich.

It was entirely selfless and with the supreme object of enriching others. This is spiritual giving.

In the days of the American Revolutionary War there lived at Ephrata, Pennsylvania a Baptist pastor by the name of Peter Miller who enjoyed the friendship of Gen. George Washington. Also residing in that town was Michael Wittman, an evil-minded man who did all in his power to abuse and oppose this pastor. One day Michael Wittman was involved in treason and was arrested and sentenced to death. The old preacher started out on foot and walked many miles to Philadelphia to plead for this man's life. He was admitted into Washington's presence and at once begged for the life of the traitor. "No, Peter," said Washington, "I cannot grant you the life of your friend." "My friend!" exclaimed the preacher, "he is the bitterest enemy I have." "What?" cried Washington, "you have walked all these miles to save the life of an enemy? That puts the matter in a different light. I will grant the pardon." And he did. And Peter Miller took Michael Wittman from the very shadow of death, back to his own home in Ephrata—no longer as an enemy, but as a friend.[2]

This is what Jesus did for you and me in His self-giving. He had no interests other than His Father's glory and our salvation and enrichment.

---

2. Adapted from *Knight's Master Book of New Illustrations* compiled by Walter B. Knight. Copyright © 1956, Eerdmans, pp. 183-184. Used by permission.

We have seen the highest example of giving in the self-emptying of our Savior; we have observed the same spirit of sacrifice, spontaneity, and spirituality in the giving of the Macedonians. Can we do any less? A thousand times no! With all our spiritual blessings and material benefits we are committed to such giving without reserve and without regret. Our song and prayer must ever be:

> When I survey the wondrous cross,
> On which the Prince of glory died,
> My richest gain I count but loss,
> And pour contempt on all my pride.
>
> Were the whole realm of nature mine,
> That were a present far too small;
> Love so amazing, so divine
> Demands my soul, my life, my all.
>
> Isaac Watts

4

The Ethics
of Giving

> And in this I give my advice: It is to your advantage not
> only to be doing what you began and were desiring to do
> a year ago; but now you also must complete the doing of
> it; that as there was a readiness to desire it, so there also
> may be a completion out of what you have.
>
> For if there is first a willing mind, it is accepted according
> to what one has, and not according to what he does not have.
>
> For I do not mean that others should be eased and you
> burdened; but by an equality, that now at this time your
> abundance may supply their lack, that their abundance also
> may supply your lack—that there may be equality.
>
> As it is written, He who gathered much had nothing left
> over, and he who gathered little had no lack.
>
> 2 Corinthians 8:10-15

Having warmed the hearts of the Corinthians with the
example of the Macedonian saints' sacrificial, spontaneous,
and spiritual giving, and also the sacrifice of our Lord Jesus
Christ, Paul proceeds to deal with the ethics of giving. He is
well aware that in no other area of life is corruption more
possible than in the handling of money. Recall, for instance,
his solemn words to Timothy: "But those who desire to be

45

rich fall into temptation and a snare, and into many foolish
and harmful lusts which drown men in destruction and
perdition. For the love of money is a root of all kinds of evil"
(1 Tim. 6:9, 10). While the gaining of money can be a curse
to the Christian, so can the giving of money; thus the need
for the ethics of giving.

There Must be Integrity in Giving

"In this I give my advice: It is to your advantage not only
to be doing what you began and were desiring to do a year
ago; but now you also must complete the doing of it; that as
there was a readiness to desire it, so there also may be a
completion out of what you have." With consummate tact,
Paul gives his advice to a church that had failed to keep a
promise and a timetable in their giving. Such behavior had
endangered their integrity. What a word this is for us today!
How easy it is for dishonesty and delay to mar and hinder
our Christian responsibility in giving!

Honesty in Keeping our Pledge to God

*It is to your advantage...to be doing what you began....
now...complete the doing of it.*

Paul was saying that it was morally imperative for their
performance to catch up and match up with the vows and
pledges that they had made. It appears that the Corinthian
church was one of the first to hear of the need in Jerusalem
and to offer help. In fact, Paul had used their enthusiastic
promise of financial assistance to challenge the churches of
Macedonia: "Your zeal has stirred up the majority" (2 Cor.
9:2). However, the Corinthians had failed in not keeping their
pledge to God, while the Macedonians had excelled
themselves in liberality out of "deep poverty" (2 Cor. 8:2).

Making a vow and then breaking it is a serious thing.
Consider what God says about this: "When you make a vow
to God, do not delay to pay it; for He has no pleasure in fools.
Pay what you have vowed. It is better not to vow than to vow
and not pay....Why should God be angry at your excuse and
destroy the work of your hands?" (Eccles. 5:4-6). God expects

us to make pledges and keep them. A pledge is a promise to God and we must believe that God will help us to fulfill it. So many people say that they are afraid to commit themselves in giving, lest they should fail God. Surely that is not only a lack of faith but also a lack of discipline, careful planning, and common sense. As someone has pointed out, we live on the principle of pledging every day of our lives. We use electric power on the basis of the pledge to pay for it monthly. We use the telephone on the basis of a pledge. We use every utility we have on the basis of a pledge and think nothing of it. And yet in God's work we say that we dare not risk a pledge. We do not credit God with the wisdom and understanding to make allowances for sicknesses and circumstances beyond our control. We think of Him only as an unbending creditor who will hold us to pledges that we cannot keep. This kind of attitude only reveals the low concept we have of our pledge to God. We need to ask the Holy Spirit to teach us integrity in giving.

My heart was greatly encouraged when this honesty in giving affected an unknown donor within the fellowship of the church I was pastoring. Someone put an envelope in the collection plate with only one word on it: "Restitution." In that envelope were six $100 bills. This was honesty in keeping a trust with God. May God speak similarly to us.

Honesty in Keeping our Time with God

And in this I give my advice: It is to your advantage not only to be doing what you began and were desiring to do a year ago."

The Corinthians had pledged their offering for Jerusalem no less than twelve months previously. Quite obviously something had occurred to delay their good intentions. A study of the epistle leaves us in no doubt as to why they had failed. They had been quarreling and contending over matters which should have been settled at the cross and forgotten immediately.

How often have we pledged ourselves, our substance or our service to God, only to defer our good intentions and break our promises because of carnal preoccupations! The

Bible says, "To everything there is a season, a time for every
purpose under heaven" (Eccles. 3:1). And Paul adds, "the time
is short" (1 Cor. 7:29); and again, "redeeming the time,
because the days are evil" (Eph. 5:16). A gift loses its maximum
value to God if it is out of timing with the plan of God. To
delay until tomorrow what God expects us to do today is to
rob our act of giving of its full moral significance.

This brings up the whole question of whether or not we
should leave our giving until we have departed this life.
Someone has said that those who defer their gifts to their
deathbeds virtually say to God, "We will now give You
something that we can keep no longer." Happy, therefore, is
the man who is his own executor, giving in life, not waiting
until death. Think of the uncounted millions of dollars in the
hands of Christian men and women that are withheld from
Christian service until death releases these vast resources. A
study of the New Testament raises questions about the wisdom
and rightness of this kind of giving. That is not to say that we
are to be irresponsible for our daily expenses, for the Scripture
says, "Owe no one anything" (Rom. 13:8). Nor does it mean
that we are not to lay up for our dependents, for the Word
of God declares, "If anyone does not provide for his own, and
especially for those of his household, he has denied the faith
and is worse than an unbeliever" (1 Tim. 5:8). Having taken
these matters into consideration, however, we should
remember that God's timetable requires our resources now,
not only after death. What is more, it is doubtful whether we
shall be rewarded for what happens after we pass from the
scene. When the apostle speaks of recompense at the
judgment seat of Christ he states that we are to be reviewed
for "the things done in the body" (2 Cor. 5:10). This means,
of course, actions taken while we are still alive and responsible.

It is incumbent upon us, as believers, to be faithful in the
management of all worldly goods committed to our trust
(1 Cor. 4:2). This includes the final disposition of our goods
and adequate provision for our loved ones (Isa. 38:1; 1 Cor.
14:40). Undoubtedly, the best way to discharge this weighty
obligation is to have a valid will. Without a will no one can
have assurance that loved ones will receive the care that was
intended. The law of intestacy follows prescribed legal

procedures which rarely coincide with the true wishes of the one who dies intestate (without a will). Thus not one penny of such an estate would go to any Christian agency for the spread of the gospel. The law does not honor good intentions! We must not allow procrastination or neglect to fail God or bring loss to our families. We must pray earnestly about the final disposition of our estate, realizing that our final accounting is not to our families or friends, but to Him with whom we are going to spend eternity. Simply stated, therefore, it is important to have a will. Make sure you see your lawyer who can draw up the necessary papers to dispose of your assets so as to provide for loved ones and Christian ministries[1]. A good lawyer would be familiar with the laws of the state in which you reside.

So you see that integrity is not only the matter of honesty in keeping our pledge to God, but also honesty in keeping our *time* with God. These Corinthians were a year late, and Paul was writing to remind them solemnly of this.

There is another aspect to our subject:

There Must Be Ability in Giving

"For if there is first a willing mind, it is accepted according to what one has, and not according to what he does not have." The sense of the text leads us to believe that God holds all men and women responsible for their measure of ability to give. Or to put it in another form, the test of generosity and faithfulness in our giving is not our wealth, but rather our willingness to give what we have. That is why Paul emphasizes, "If there is first a willing mind, it is accepted according to what one has, and not according to what he does not have."

Richard Foster was exuberant when his six-year-old son came home from school and asked if he could give his lunch box to a classmate because the other child had need of one. Foster's response: "Hallelujah!"[2]

---

1. Such ministries should bear the emblem of the Evangelical Council for Financial Accountability—the symbol of trust.
2. Richard Foster, *Celebration of Discipline* (New York: Harper & Row, 1978), p. 79, adapted.

Dr. Roy L. Laurin puts it perfectly when he says, "If you give a dollar, and someone gives one hundred dollars, the smallness of your gift would not be measured by the largeness of the other person's gift. The measurement would be according to what you have and the willingness with which you gave what you had."[3]

Intent in the Ability of Giving

For if there is first a willing mind, it is accepted."

This matter of intent cannot be overemphasized. Mark Twain quipped that when some men discharge an obligation, you can hear the report for miles around. There are many people who give merely to maintain their reputation or to silence the voice of conscience; but what pleases God is the spontaneous intention of a willing mind. The Hebrew writer says, "Do not forget to do good and to share, for with such sacrifices God is well pleased" (Heb. 13:16). If the clear intention to give is already in the heart the amount is of secondary importance. The sacrifice which pleases the heart of God is the willingness of mind to give in response to the greatest gift of all, the Lord Jesus Christ.

This aspect of truth is beautifully demonstrated by David in his desire to build a temple (1 Sam. 7). He wished to express his love for God in the form of a sanctuary in which the law of God could be read and the will of God revealed. But you will remember that when David bared his heart to Jehovah he was told, "You have shed much blood and have made great wars; you shall not build a house for My name, because you have shed much blood on the earth in My sight" (1 Chron. 22:8). So David was given the privilege of gathering the materials, while his son, Solomon, erected the temple. The point of the story is that the intention to build a temple was in the heart of only one man—and that man was David. We need a willingness of mind, both in regard to our responsibility and our privilege in giving.

---

3. Roy L. Laurin, *II Corinthians: Where Life Endures,* pp. 165-166.

Extent in the Ability of Giving

Accepted according to what one has, and not according to what he does not have.

What is your attitude toward your financial responsibilities? Someone has well said that responsibility, for Christians, is our response to God's ability. There are five possible attitudes: 1) We may shirk our responsibilities; 2) We may shelve them, hoping that at some time or other we may fulfill them; 3) We may shoulder them, and wear ourselves out bearing their full weight; 4) We may shed them after having made an attempt to fulfill them; or 5) We may share them. It is the fifth course of action that best fulfills the law of Christ and brings glory to God.

In summing up the ethics involved in the ability to give we do well to recall the story of Ananias and Sapphira (Acts 5). Peter made it very plain, in addressing Ananias, that while their joint estate remained it was their own. After it was sold it was in their power or ability to give as God should guide them. God's purpose is never to press us to give what we cannot, but only that which we are able. The failure in the case of these two was in their intent. They agreed to give part of the price in the name of the whole, and for this unethical procedure they were judged with the stroke of death. We must determine that in all our ministry of giving we are absolutely ethical in both the intent and extent of ability in giving.

There Must Be Equality in Giving

"For I do not mean that others should be eased and you burdened; but by an equality...your abundance may supply their lack, that their abundance also may supply your lack....As it is written, 'He who gathered much had nothing left over, and he who gathered little had no lack.'" The Bible teaches that no believer has a right to enjoy this world's goods while his brother is in need. This explains why the church functioned as it did in those early days of persecution and privation. After Pentecost, because of distress and need, "all who believed...had all things in common, and sold their possessions and goods, and divided them among all, as anyone had need" (Acts 2:44-45). Such teaching does not in any way support either the Marxist idea of communism or the kind of giving which encourages luxury or laziness.

In Prosperity We are to Relieve the Needs of Others

By an equality...your abundance may supply their lack.

John teaches exactly the same principle when he says with searching penetration, "Whoever has this world's goods, and sees his brother in need, and shuts up his heart from him, how does the love of God abide in him?" (1 John 3:17). This concept of equality, of course, applies not only to people in need, but also to situations that require financial assistance.

In our generation the great proportion of giving in our churches is directed to such causes as missions, radio, television, social services, and other ministries for reaching and helping the lost. While we are able to support such endeavors we are committed to do so. This is equality in giving. Paul warns, however, that equality in giving should not cause the saints in Jerusalem to be eased, while others are burdened. The Jerusalem saints were not to enjoy plush seats while the Corinthian Christians sat on hard benches! On the contrary, there should be wisdom and a sense of balance in this whole matter of sharing the resources of a local church.

Then Paul takes pains to show that the reverse is just as true.

In Adversity We are to Receive the Gifts of Others

Their abundance also may supply your lack—that there may be equality.

Some people will not accept gifts lest they should be obligated to the donors. This, in Paul's view, is unethical. We should receive all that God gives us through our brethren with a holy sense of gratefulness since the time may well come when we have to reciprocate by showing the kindness shown to us. This truth was not for Corinth only; it is relevant today.

When we think of reciprocating, too many of us think in terms of repaying our benefactor. Perhaps recalling an occasion in the life of D. L. Moody will give us a different perspective. Once, when Mr. Moody was in New York, he was helped tremendously by R. K. Remington. As he was leaving on the train, Mr. Moody grasped his friend by the hand and said, "If you ever come to Chicago, call on me and I will try to return your kindness." Mr. Remington replied, "Don't wait for me; do it to the first man that comes along."[4]

The fortunes of life change very quickly. Today we may have abundance while tomorrow we may be in want. Today we may live in luxury while tomorrow we may be experiencing lack. Today we may have the privilege of giving while tomorrow we may have the equal privilege of receiving. So equality in giving teaches that the rich are not to be expected to bear all the load, and the poor are not to be excused from proportionate responsibility.

To illustrate his point, Paul cites an incident in Israel's history (Exod. 16:18). It was the case of an Israelite who went out to gather manna. Overcome with greed, he appropriated more than was his portion and found that the residue turned into a foul mass of pollution. On the other hand, the individual who gathered less than was his due had no lack.

So God levels all His people to the point of equal rights in His presence. If we fail to give in prosperity God will curse what we hold back. In the same way, if we fail to receive in adversity God will judge us for the pride that hinders us from recognizing His providing hand.

Here, then, is the challenge of the ethics of giving. The more we study this passage, the more it becomes clear that Paul has covered the whole ground of *morality* in the matter of money. To take these principles to heart is to please God and to live in blessing; to reject them is to break the heart of God and to fall into "temptation and a snare" which may lead to "destruction and perdition" (1 Tim. 6:9). God expects integrity, ability, and equality in our giving. When we have fulfilled His will we realize that we have not done God a favor

---

4. Harold Lindsell, *My Daily Quiet Time* (Grand Rapids: Zondervan, 1969), p. 81, adapted.

but rather followed what is right. "For God is not unjust to forget your work and labor of love which you have shown toward His name, in that you have ministered to the saints, and do minister" (Heb. 6:10).

A farmer was known for his generous giving, but his friends could not understand how he could give so much away and yet remain so prosperous. One day a spokesman for his friends said, "We cannot understand you. You give far more than the rest of us and yet you always seem to have more to give." "Oh, that is easy to explain," the farmer said. "I keep shoveling into God's bin and God keeps shoveling into mine, but God has the bigger shovel!" Here was a man whose ethics of giving were controlled by the power of an indwelling Lord.

Who controls your finances? Is it self or is your testimony something like this?

> I'm feeling very rich today,
> For Jesus holds my purse.
> I need not count its scanty store
> As all the assets at my door;
> Behind it stands a wealthy name,
> And vast resources I may claim
> Since Jesus holds my purse.
>
> My Cashier never lets me want;
> Since He controls my purse
> Debit and credit always meet.
> I marvel at His counsel sweet
> Concerning purchases I make,
> Or money given for His dear sake,
> While He controls my purse.
>
> I'd face the world in great alarm
> If Judas held my purse.
> He'd call the gifts of humble love
> Naught but a waste; treasure above
> Uncertain quantity and poor.
> My life would barren be, I'm sure,
> If Judas held my purse.
>
> And thus I live a carefree life
> For Jesus holds my purse.

Since money is a sacred thing,
Both joy and sorrow it may bring
According as we do His will,
Or find our hearts rebellious still.
Let Jesus hold your purse.

Selected

5

The Efficiency
of Giving

But thanks be to God who puts the same earnest care for you into the heart of Titus. For he not only accepted the exhortation, but being more diligent, he went to you of his own accord.

And we have sent with him the brother whose praise is in the gospel throughout all the churches, and not only that, but who was also chosen by the churches to travel with us with this gift, which is administered by us to the glory of the Lord Himself and to show your ready mind, avoiding this: that anyone should blame us in this lavish gift which is administered by us—providing honorable things, not only in the sight of the Lord, but also in the sight of men.

And we have sent with them our brother whom we have often proved diligent in many things, but now much more diligent, because of the great confidence which we have in you.

If anyone inquires about Titus, he is my partner and fellow worker concerning you. Or if our brethren are inquired about, they are messengers of the churches, the glory of Christ. Therefore show to them, and before the churches, the proof of your love and of our boasting on your behalf.

Now concerning the ministering to the saints, it is superfluous for me to write to you; for I know your willingness, about which I boast of you to the Macedonians, that Achaia was ready a year ago; and your zeal has stirred up the majority.

> Yet I have sent the brethren, lest our boasting of you should be in vain in this respect, that, as I said, you may be ready; lest if some Macedonians come with me and find you unprepared, we (not to mention you!) should be ashamed of this confident boasting.
>
> Therefore I thought it necessary to exhort the brethren to go to you ahead of time, and prepare your bountiful gift beforehand, which you had previously promised, that it may be ready as a matter of generosity and not as a grudging obligation.
>
> 2 Corinthians 8:16—9:5

In our last chapter we discussed the ethics of giving. Paul announces and applies these principles with solemn authority. But now in the process of logical development he deals with a matter which calls for equal consideration and implementation in the local church: the question of the efficiency of giving. The apostle is saying that there is no point in exhorting God's people to give generously and ethically if the management of their gifts lacks efficiency. Church members— and particularly officers—are responsible to God for honesty in the handling of money and wisdom in the dispensing of it. The verses before us deal with two main considerations:

The Motivation of Efficient Giving

"Providing honorable things, not only in the sight of the Lord, but also in the sight of men." Paul confronts his readers with a twofold motivation which should determine not only Christian giving, but also Christian living.

The Glory of God

This gift, which is administered by us to the glory of the Lord.

He touched on this motivation in his first letter to the Corinthians, where he says, "Whatever you do, do all to the glory of God" (1 Cor. 10:31). Anything less than fulfilling the will of God to the glory of God is defined in Holy Scripture as sin, "for all have sinned and fall short of the glory of God" (Rom. 3:23).

What is more, the Westminster Catechism makes it clear that "Man's chief end is to glorify God and to enjoy Him forever." We are to glorify God by our worshipful praise: "Whoever offers praise glorifies Me" (Ps. 50:23). We are to glorify Him by our consistent fruitbearing: "By this My Father is glorified, that you bear much fruit" (John 15:8). We are to glorify Him by our spiritual unity: "that you may with one mind and one mouth glorify the God and Father of our Lord Jesus Christ" (Rom. 15:6). We are to glorify Him by our entire dedication: "For you were bought at a price; therefore glorify God in your body and in your spirit, which are God's" (1 Cor. 6:20). And we are to glorify Him by our good works: "Let your light so shine before men, that they may see your good works and glorify your Father in heaven" (Matt. 5:16). In this last category is included the matter of giving. Only in this way can we provide for "honorable things...in the sight of the Lord." The glory of God should motivate us to give—and to give our best.

Queen Mary was walking in the vicinity of Balmoral, Scotland on a dark and cloudy day. She strolled rather far, and as the rain came down she stopped at a cottage for the loan of an umbrella. The woman did not recognize the Queen, so she decided to give the stranger an old umbrella with a broken rib. The next morning a man in gold braid appeared at the cottage door. "The Queen asked me to thank you for lending her the umbrella," he explained. The woman in the cottage was dumbfounded and with tears flowing down her cheeks said, "What an opportunity I missed! Why did I not give the Queen the best umbrella I had?"

The Good of Man

Providing honorable things, not only in the sight of the Lord, but also in the sight of men.

Paul amplifies and explains this concept in the previous verse where he says, "Avoiding this: that anyone should blame us in this lavish gift which is administered by us." Paul recognized how important it was that the contributions of the churches, both in Macedonia and Corinth, for the poor saints in Jerusalem should be handled with scrupulous care, so that neither he nor his associates would be open to the slightest suspicion of misappropriating other people's money.

What an example the apostle has left us! It is so easy for Christian people to suppose that as long as they have an unclouded conscience regarding their acts before God it does not matter whether or not they appear honest before their fellow men. In every fellowship of God's people there is the temptation to minimize the importance of making church actions transparent before others, so that all activity is beyond suspicion. One theologian has said, "It is a foolish pride which leads to a disregard of public opinion." Both Old and New Testaments corroborate this principle. Solomon says, "A false balance is an abomination to the Lord, but a just weight is His delight" (Prov. 11:1). The apostle Paul adds, "Have regard for good [or honest] things in the sight of all men" (Rom. 12:17).

Dr. G. Campbell Morgan recalls that when the Salvation Army started its work General William Booth was charged with dishonesty. People said that all the property was in his name and that he at any time might have converted that property into money and appropriated it for himself. However, from the very beginning, Booth was careful to publish his accounts, and over the years that criticism ceased entirely.

The same thing happened in the ministry of Dr. Billy Graham. Both in this country and overseas he was accused of conducting his crusades for personal gain; but wisely and scripturally he saw to it that reputable accountants in each city published all facts and figures relating to a crusade. Furthermore, he insisted on putting himself and the other members of his team on salary.

Many other instances could be cited to illustrate this basic principle of the church of "providing honorable things, not only in the sight of the Lord, but also in the sight of men."

The Ministration of Efficient Giving

"Avoiding this: that anyone should blame us in this lavish

gift which is administered by us." No one in the Corinthian church could ever accuse Paul of being impracticable or inefficient. He was forever relating the highest concepts of theology to the business of everyday living. This is particularly true of the verses we are now studying. He has just dealt with the serious theme of the ethics of giving. Now he proceeds to discuss the efficiency of giving. He says that the motivation of giving must be linked with the ministration of giving.

The Engagement of Efficient Men

But thanks be to God who puts the same earnest care for you into the heart of Titus....And we have sent with him the brother whose praise is in the gospel throughout all the churches....We have sent with them our brother whom we have often proved diligent in many things.

No one can study these verses without being deeply impressed by the care with which Paul handled this matter of the engagement of efficient men. Titus was obviously his own choice, his "partner and fellow worker." The other two unnamed brethren were the appointees of the churches involved in the giving.

Titus, though not mentioned in the Acts, was one of Paul's very close companions and a man in whom Paul had put a considerable amount of trust. As we have seen, he refers to him as "my partner and fellow worker." Titus had already been to Corinth and, in fact, had been responsible for the delicate task of smoothing over the tense situation which had arisen between Paul and the Corinthians. He was, therefore, a man of great tact and force of character. Even more important, he was a leader who possessed great ability as an administrator. Although his primary ministry in the church at Corinth was a spiritual one, it is clear from the reading of chapters 8 and 9 of 2 Corinthians that he was also responsible for organizing the money-raising program. So Paul asked him to return, accompanied by this very letter, to complete the task of collecting the necessary financial assistance for the saints in Jerusalem.

The second brother mentioned is unnamed, though many believe he may have been Barnabas, John Mark, Luke, or even

Apollos! What is said about him, however, is very beautiful
and commendable. He was evidently well known to the
Corinthians for his praiseworthy evangelistic ministry
throughout all the churches. Notice what Paul says, "And we
have sent...the brother whose praise is in the gospel
throughout all the churches." This man obviously had a
redemptive passion for the lost. One can visualize his children
in the faith in the congregations across Macedonia and also
in the church at Corinth.

The third brother referred to is also unnamed. He, too, is
highly commended, for Paul declares, "We have...often proved
[him] diligent in many things." W. C. G. Proctor, in his little
commentary on II Corinthians, writes: "If we allow ourselves
a little liberty, we may think of this brother as a Christian
accountant...who allied his accountancy with evangelism." His
diligence suggests that he was particularly capable and reliable
in matters financial.

We know that Titus was a pastoral administrator, the first
unnamed brother was a praiseworthy evangelist, and the
second unnamed man was a proficient accountant. But what
is supremely important is that all three were men of God.
Surely we have to give the apostle unqualified credit for his
discernment in the choice of these men. No wonder he could
conclude his commendation of his brethren with the glorious
words, "they are messengers of the churches, the glory of
Christ. Therefore show to them, and before the churches, the
proof of your love and of our boasting on your behalf."

Thoughtful people agree that here is the ministration of
efficient giving at its best. This is management at its loftiest.
Such teaching contrasts with the sloppy and slovenly way
money matters are handled in many of our modern churches!
The usual democratic procedure of accepting anyone, so long
as he or she is elected by the church, certainly does not tally
with this apostolic standard. Let us emphasize that these were
men of manifest spirituality, maturity, and recognized ability.

Note that for administering the large sums of money which
had been collected, Paul insisted on having at least three
outstanding men. In this he was following a scriptural
principle which is to be found in both Old and New Testaments

—one which he particularly emphasizes in the closing paragraphs of the epistle we are studying: "By the mouth of two or three witnesses every word shall be established" (2 Cor. 13:1). So we see the importance of engaging efficient men for the high and holy task of handling money in the life of the church.

This biblical principle of management has been used with great efficiency in a time of international crisis. During World War II the Spartan Aircraft Company received a contract to manufacture a component of a fighter bomber wing assembly. The "experts" said it would take eighteen months to gear up for production and four hundred man-hours to produce each component. With a war on, this seemed like an eternity. Spartan's management team asked the employees for their ideas on how to cut preparation time and how to reduce the man-hours required to manufacture each component. Using the ideas of their employees, the company was in full production in eight months, using only forty man-hours to make each part of the wing assembly. So, too, in the church, we must never overlook the importance of efficient men.[1]

The Employment of Efficient Methods

In this I give my advice (2 Cor. 8:10);....Now concerning the ministering to the saints, it is superfluous for me to write to you....Yet I have sent the brethren.

These three statements make it apparent that the apostle had a method for raising money, both for local and general needs.

Scriptural Indoctrination

When Paul speaks of giving advice he is not offering his own opinion; he is pressing his exhortation on the basis of sound biblical principles already laid down. Perhaps the essence of his teaching is best summed up in a verse that we have previously considered: "On the first day of the week let each one of you lay something aside, storing up as he may

---

1. Myron Rush, *Management: A Biblical Approach* (Wheaton: Victor, 1983), p. 22, adapted.

prosper, that there be no collections when I come" (1 Cor. 16:2). What Paul has said here and elsewhere is that giving to God should be more than an emotional exercise; it should be the expression of a theological conviction. This, of course, is the direct opposite of the psychological tricks and carnal pressures that are often employed today.

Pastoral Communication

He had already written "concerning the collection" (1 Cor. 16:1), and now he communicates with them again. In fact, the two chapters that we are presently considering are the fullest treatment on the grace of giving that we have in the New Testament. Most of what is written, however, is in the form of a pastoral exhortation and is, therefore, a guide for all whose task it is to stir up God's people to fulfill their stewardship responsibilities. So whether by letter or personal exhortation, the pastor of a church has an apostolic precedent to follow in challenging Christians to give. We are certainly to trust God to meet our needs, but we are also to inform His people and to provide them with an opportunity to test the sincerity of their love (2 Cor. 8:8).

Official Administration

Paul says, "Yet I have sent the brethren." We know these men were eminently suited for their task, but we should also observe that they had an official mandate to administer the offerings. These chosen men, because of scriptural teaching and pastoral exhortation, were free to collect the gifts from the church treasury, determine a reckoning of them, and then prepare the gifts for transportation to Jerusalem. In effect, their task was to see that individual members, as well as the church corporate, were following through on their financial responsibilities. Thank God for every local church that has a board of deacons "of good reputation, full of the Holy Spirit and wisdom" (Acts 6:3; 1 Tim. 3:8-13) who are able to challenge the membership concerning these matters and also to give adequate advice on Christian giving. It is a sad situation when the responsibility is left entirely to the pastor.

We have seen that in money matters, as in all other aspects

of church life, we are expected to do "all things...decently and in order" (1 Cor. 14:40). Let us then ever bear in mind the true motivation of efficient giving and be careful to follow through on the ministration of efficient giving. Only in this way shall we glorify God and edify the church.

6

The Enrichment
of Giving

But this I say: He who sows sparingly will also reap sparingly, and he who sows bountifully will also reap bountifully.

So let each one give as he purposes in his heart, not grudgingly or of necessity; for God loves a cheerful giver.

And God is able to make all grace abound toward you, that you, always having all sufficiency in all things, have an abundance for every good work. As it is written: He has dispersed abroad, He has given to the poor; His righteousness remains forever.

Now may He who supplies seed to the sower, and bread for food, supply and multiply the seed you have sown and increase the fruits of your righteousness, while you are enriched in everything for all liberality, which causes thanksgiving through us to God.

For the administration of this service not only supplies the needs of the saints, but also is abounding through many thanksgivings to God, while, through the proof of this ministry, they glorify God for the obedience of your confession to the gospel of Christ, and for your liberal sharing with them and all men, and by their prayer for you, who long for you because of the exceeding grace of God in you.

Thanks be to God for His indescribable gift!

2 Corinthians 9:6-15

In this final paragraph of 2 Corinthians 9 Paul climaxes his treatment of the grace of giving with some weighty words on the enriching ministry of Christian giving. He is determined to impress on his readers the all-important fact that the grace of giving is God's supreme method of enriching those who dispense gifts as well as those who receive gifts. So he speaks in these verses of four important matters.

The Enrichment of Fruitfulness in Giving

"But this I say: He who sows sparingly will also reap sparingly, and he who sows bountifully will also reap bountifully." The laws of harvest operate not only in the natural, but also in the spiritual realm. Paul illustrates this fact by drawing attention to the farmer who sows his spring crop. The farmer knows that what he has sown in the spring he will harvest in the fall. One of those unalterable laws states that he will reap what he has sown. Moreover, the farmer understands that the proportion of his reaping will be determined by the proportion of his sowing. If he is foolish enough to sow sparingly he will reap sparingly; on the other hand, if he is wise enough to sow bountifully he will also reap bountifully. This principle is operative in all areas of Christian experience, and especially in the area of giving. The believer recognizes that giving is not a question of scattering, but of sowing. It is not a contribution; it is an investment. All giving constitutes a challenge to our faith. No farmer sows without exercising a simple faith in the law of harvest. If he had no faith he would not sow at all. In his Letter to the Galatians Paul speaks specifically of this enrichment of fruitfulness in giving:

> Do not be deceived, God is not mocked; for whatever a man sows, that he will also reap. For he who sows to his flesh will of the flesh reap corruption, but he who sows to the Spirit will of the Spirit reap everlasting life. And let us not grow weary while doing good, for in due season we shall reap if we do not lose heart (Gal. 6:7-9).

In this passage, which is primaily associated with the subject of giving, the apostle shows that there are two kinds of sowing which result in two kinds of reaping.

A *Carnal Harvest*

He who sows to his flesh will of the flesh reap corruption (Gal. 6:8).

There is no enrichment in this kind of giving. A carnal Christian sows to the flesh by spending resources to gratify personal desires. Such a person must expect nothing less than the reaping of corruption. That which might have been rewarded by being invested in the Lord's work will be nothing but "wood, hay, [and] straw" (1 Cor. 3:12-15). Careful thought reveals that this matter of carnal giving impinges on motives as well as means, for it is not only what we give but how we give and why we give that matters in the presence of God.

A *Spiritual Harvest*

He who sows to the Spirit will of the Spirit reap everlasting life (Gal. 6:8).

Here is the enrichment of fruitfulness in giving which is available to all who will venture out in faith in the ministry of giving. The text actually means that as we respond to the indwelling Spirit in love and sacrifice we shall be adding interest to the capital of eternal life which we already have in Christ. Nobody can merit the gift of eternal life by personal works of righteousness, "for by grace you have been saved through faith, and that not of yourselves; it is the gift of God, not of works, lest anyone should boast" (Eph. 2:8-9).

But having made that clear, we must recognize that there is a whole body of Scripture which reveals that we can add to our spiritual capital by a continuing enrichment through the ministry of giving. In fact, there is no area of Christian experience which deepens the capacity for more of the gifts of God than that of sacrificial giving. Introduce me to a niggardly Christian and I will show you a person whose Christian life is shriveled up. On the other hand, lead me to a believer who knows the joy of sacrificial giving and I will point out a person whose life is one of fruitful enrichment. I am convinced that the devil has caused the subject of giving to stir up resistance and resentment among God's people because he knows there are few ways of spiritual enrichment like the exercise of Christian giving.

C.S. Lewis didn't talk about percentage giving. He said the only safe rule is to give more than we can spare. Our charities should pinch and hamper us. If we live at the same level of affluence as other people who have our level of income, we are probably giving away too little.[1]

Let us never forget that at the very heart of the gospel is the whole principle of giving. Heaven could never be enriched with the company of the redeemed if Jesus had not given Himself, even to the death of the cross. By the same token, we can never enrich the church or our personal lives without sacrificial stewardship. There is no fruitfulness without the ministry of giving.

The Enrichment of Joyfulness in Giving

"Let each one give as he purposes in his heart, not grudgingly or of necessity; for God loves a cheerful giver." Giving develops a capacity not only for fruitfulness but also for joyfulness. Misery is always linked with miserliness, whereas merriment is indissolubly associated with magnanimity. To know such joyfulness, however, Paul says that giving must be exercised without casualness—"Let each one give as he purposes in his heart." This takes us back to principles we have already considered. God has given careful instruction as to how we should develop holy habits of laying "something aside...as he may prosper" (1 Cor. 16:2) so we can give out of a true sense of purpose and planning. Casualness implies carelessness and heartlessness and, therefore, joylessness. The very discipline which determines a sense of purpose is the discipline which deepens joy in our Christian experience.

---
1. Kathryn Ann Lindskoog, "True Charity," in *Hymns for the Family of God* (Nashville: Abingdon, 1976), p. 514.

Furthermore, we are to give without complaint—"not grudgingly." Here is a searing word to all our hearts. Many among us must confess that when the challenge of stewardship has come we experience a spirit of unwillingness and even rebellion. There is no joy in this and, therefore, no enrichment. May God enable us to bring our unwillingness to give what God demands and deserves to the cross until the joy of giving is born in our souls.

Once again in our text we are told to give without compulsion—"There should be no reluctance, no sense of compulsion; God loves a cheerful giver" (NEB). The believer must not be more concerned by what others will think of him if he refrains from giving. Sad to say, much giving is motivated by the safeguarding of our good name, and such unworthy thoughts rob Christian giving of its loveliness and joy. God's purpose is rather that we should experience the enrichment of joyfulness in giving. He says, "Let each one give as he purposes in his heart, not grudgingly or of necessity; for God loves a cheerful giver." As we have been reminded so often, the word *cheerful* here can be rendered "hilarious," suggesting a spirit of real enjoyment which sweeps away all human restraints. The Lord Jesus summed up this enrichment of joyfulness in giving when He said, "It is more blessed to give than to receive" (Acts 20:35). This astonishing statement is not found in the Gospels, and yet Paul uses it in his address to the elders at Ephesus to press home the enrichment which comes through the sacrifice of giving. He says, in effect, that if only these brethren would learn the deep principle of joy through giving their lives would be truly blessed. In every local church of Jesus Christ there are people who can testify to the outworking of this spiritual law in their lives. They never knew what it was to be joyful until they learned how to give without casualness, complaint or compulsion.

A lovely story is told of the saintly Frances Ridley Havergal who wrote the lines we so often sing without due seriousness and commitment:

> Take my silver and my gold,
> Not a mite would I withhold.

It is a matter of record that this hymn was autobiographical. Frances Ridley Havergal did what she sang. In her writings is this personal testimony: "'Take my silver and my gold' now means shipping off all my ornaments—including a jewel cabinet which is really fit for a countess—to the Church Missionary Society....I don't think I need to tell you I never packed a box with such pleasure." This was giving with hilarity!

The Enrichment of Usefulness in Giving

"And God is able to make all grace abound toward you, that you, always having all sufficiency in all things, have an abundance for every good work....Now may He who supplies seed to the sower, and bread for food, supply and multiply the seed you have sown and increase the fruits of your righteousness." The miracle of giving is that it produces a ministry of giving. When God can trust His people with money, He sees to it that they always have plenty for themselves and more for others. So the apostle quotes Psalm 112:9 to support this divine principle: "He hath dispersed abroad, he has given to the poor; his righteousness endures forever; his horn will be exalted with honor." There is honor and reward where generosity has been exercised. God is no man's debtor. Simply stated, this law of enrichment of usefulness in giving works as follows:

God Meets Our Requirements

He...supplies seed to the sower, and bread for food.

The God of Elijah is still the same today. When Elijah put himself at God's disposal he never lacked anything, even though the land was scourged with famine. Even when the brook Cherith dried up and the ravens ceased to bring his daily meal, God provided his daily bread (1 Kings 17). Later David testified, "I have been young, and now am old; yet I have not seen the righteous forsaken, nor his descendants begging bread" (Ps. 37:25). When Jesus was on earth He challenged His disciples with the words, "'When I sent you without money bag, sack, and sandals, did you lack anything?' So they said, 'Nothing'" (Luke 22:35). The apostle Paul sums it up when he says, "I have learned in whatever state I am, to be content: I know how to be abased, and I know how to abound. Everywhere and in all things I have learned both to be full and to be hungry, both to abound and to suffer need" (Phil. 4:11-12); and again, "My God shall supply all your need" (Phil. 4:19).

God Multiplies Our Resources

Now may He who supplies seed to the sower, and bread for food, supply and multiply the seed you have sown.

God alone is responsible for the measure in which these resources are multiplied, for the promise is clear and sure: He multiplies the seed that is sown. Giving is not self-impoverishment but self-enrichment. The Lord Jesus affirms that giving is an assurance of gaining: "Give, and it will be given to you: good measure, pressed down, shaken together, and running over will be put into your bosom. For with the same measure that you use, it will be measured back to you" (Luke 6:38). This, of course, must not be our motive for giving lest, as someone has said, "we vitiate the whole ethical value of the act. But our Lord offers this assurance, that giving is never a one-way street: it is the door to plenty."

Scores of examples could be cited to show how God multiplies the resources of those who give in the right measure and with the right motive.

As a young man, Robert Laidlaw made a covenant with God that he would give a tenth of all his earnings. Later, at the age of twenty-five, he decided to change that amount to fifty percent of all his earnings. God continued to multiply his resources until he was giving even more to the work of the Lord. Writing at the age of seventy, he said: "I want to bear testimony that, in spiritual communion and in material things, God has blessed me one hundredfold, and has graciously entrusted to me a stewardship far beyond my expectations when, as a lad of eighteen, I gave God a definite portion of my wages."

The same could be related of William Colgate, who joined

a church in the city of New York. As a boy, he gave ten cents out of every dollar he earned to the Lord's work. As his business prospered he increased his giving—first to two-tenths and finally reaching five-tenths. Then when his children were educated he gave all his income to God.

We could mention God's prospering hand on men like Heinz, of "57 Varieties" fame; H. P. Crowell of Quaker Oats; Kraft, of Kraft Cheese; and many others. The fact that all Christians do not become famous does not alter the principle that God multiplies our actual resources when we learn how to give sacrificially to Him and His work.

The names I have just mentioned are world-famous, but the history of Christian giving has demonstrated that there are none so poor that they cannot give. There was a woman with no money and too old to work. She began to pray, "Teach me how to obtain. Give me someone to send out and support as a missionary." Before her death she was suporting ninety-three missionaries. Another, a young clerk, gave up his midmorning coffee and buns, buying tracts with the pennies saved and seeking, through these, to lead men to Christ. A husband, scarcely able to make ends meet, determined that not one penny of income would be spent until he and his wife saw to it that twenty-five cents out of every dollar were given to God. By the end of the month their business had so prospered that they increased their giving and gave a joyful testimony to the church concerning the seal that the Lord had set upon their faith and obedience. Others adopted a sliding scale of giving, steeply increasing as their incomes rose.

Timing counts, too, so our obedience must be prompt. A businessman went to a missionary society with $280 toward sending a new recruit overseas. He was told that he was too late. They had just canceled her passage for lack of the money. In tears he then confessed, "God told me to give it some days ago, but I delayed."

We must not expect to be untested in this act of faith. The patriarch Job gave generously to God (Job 1:5), and to the poor (Job 29:16); but for a time he was stripped of everything, though later he received it back again in richer measure. Then there are times when God may accept our gifts and lay them up as treasure in heaven, as He promised the rich young ruler. Some give just because they are asked, without thought as to the value of the cause; others give for secondary reasons, while some give from love of God and after careful thought.

So we would say in the words of another: "If you want to be rich, give; if you want to be poor, grasp! if you want abundance, scatter; if you want to be needy, hoard! And again:

> A man there was, and some did count him mad:
> The more he gave away, the more he had.

Selected

The Word of God supports this by saying, "There is one who scatters, yet increases more; and there is one who withholds more than is right, but it leads to poverty. The generous soul will be made rich, and he who waters will also be watered himself" (Prov. 11:24-25).

God Motivates Our Responsibility

God is able to....increase the fruits of your righteousness.

In other words, He motivates our giving and then causes our gifts to become the fruits of righteousness to others. The people and causes to which we give are not only materially blessed, but also spiritually blessed because our giving is the fruit of righteousness. This, in the highest sense, is sowing to the Spirit. It is one thing to dispense a gift; it is quite another to impart a spiritual blessing by the act of giving. We all have had experiences of this sort. There is a kind of giving which may have enriched us materially, but left us dead spiritually; there is another quality of giving which may not have enriched us materially, but has blessed us spiritually. God teach us the enrichment in giving until "our very hearts o'erflow"!

The Enrichment of Thankfulness in Giving

"You are enriched in everything for all liberality, which causes thanksgiving through us to God....Thanks be to God for His indescribable gift!" Thankfulness is the ultimate in all

Christian stewardship. When God has so worked in our hearts that giving turns to worship, then we have truly experienced the grace of giving. There is no greater evidence of a Spirit-filled person than a praising Christian. When Paul exhorts the believers at Ephesus to "be filled with the Spirit" he adds immediately, "giving thanks always for all things to God" (Eph. 5:18, 20).

In one of his vivid stories, Charles Allen says that if he were an artist, he would paint a picture showing five thousand hungry people. Standing in their midst would be Jesus, who is always concerned about human need. In His hands would be a little boy's lunch. Allen suggests that Jesus might have complained about having so little when He needed so much. Instead of complaining, He lifted up His eyes to God and gave thanks. By His example Jesus taught us to be thankful in all things.[2]

The Bible makes it plain that there is no greater enrichment of the total human personality than the spirit of thankfulness. Remember, in one of the profoundest statements we find in the New Testament, the apostle tells us that God has "predestined us...according to the good pleasure of His will, to the praise of the glory of His grace" (Eph. 1:5-6). So our chief occupation in heaven is going to be worship and praise to God.

It follows, therefore, that the enrichment of thankfulness comes by way of the ministry of giving.

Soul-satisfying

You are enriched in everything for all liberality, which causes thanksgiving through us to God.

There is nothing more satisfying in all the world than the God-given thankfulness which comes from enriching others. It is a level of thankfulness rarely found in Christians today, but it is part of God's purpose for His children. Just as His own heart was never satisfied until He had given His all to redeem mankind, so the believer can never be truly satisfied

---

2. Charles L. Wallis, ed., *The Charles L. Allen Treasury* (Old Tappan: Revell, 1970), p. 51, adapted.

until he reaches the point where living for others fills him with thanksgiving to God. Paul expresses this gratitude when he says: "I thank Christ Jesus our Lord who has enabled me, because He counted me faithful, putting me into the ministry, although I was formerly a blasphemer, a persecutor, and an insolent man" (1 Tim. 1:12-13). The supreme cause of Paul's thanksgiving was that God had delivered him from bigoted self-centeredness and religious cruelty to serve others to the glory of God.

Church-edifying

For the administration of this service not only supplies the needs of the saints, but also is abounding through many thanksgivings to God, while, through the proof of this ministry, they glorify God for the obedience of your confession to the gospel of Christ, and for your liberal sharing with them and all men.

These two verses are quite remarkable. They show how the enrichment of thankfulness in giving teaches the church to both praise and pray. Paul promises that the saints at Jerusalem will be inspired to praise God because of the liberality of the Corinthian church members. One of the greatest problems in convincing unbelievers of the reality of the gospel is that there is seldom any evidence of practical liberality. Thankfulness for the liberality of the Corinthian Christians edified the Jerusalem church not only in their ministry of praise, but also in their ministry of prayer, for Paul goes right on to say, "and by their prayer for you, who long for you because of the exceeding grace of God in you." Nothing develops the capacity for prayer in the life of a Christian as does the spirit of thanksgiving. Wherever you find thankful people you will find praying people; praise and prayer are the outstanding marks of an edified church.

God-magnifying

Thanks be to God for His indescribable gift!

This is the climax to the whole subject of giving. In this glorious doxology Paul is saying that every time we give with thankfulness we reflect the unspeakable love of God in giving His only Son for the salvation of men. Already the apostle has touched on this profound subject by declaring, "You know the grace of our Lord Jesus Christ, that though He was rich, yet for your sakes He became poor, that you through His poverty might become rich" (2 Cor. 8:9).

Here is divine giving at its highest and deepest. At its highest level we catch sight of the unmerited favor God bestows in sending His Son from heaven's glory down to earth's gloom. At its deepest level we are introduced to the unutterable poverty to which our Lord descended. Paul is so careful about this that he uses a Greek word which can be translated "pauperism." The Lord Jesus became a pauper on this earth that we might be introduced to all the riches of His grace. Now, says Paul, whenever we give, remember that we are only reflecting the self-giving of God. This should fill us with unspeakable thanksgiving to our Lord.

In the light of such teaching it is difficult to understand how any sensitive and reasonable Christian can hold back all that God demands and deserves. Who among us does not long to live a life of fruitfulness, joyfulness, usefulness, and thankfulness? Paul maintains this cannot happen—and will not happen—until we know how to give not only of ourselves and our service, but also of our substance. *The true measure of yieldedness to the lordship of Christ is the measure of our discipline and devotion in Christian giving.* We can talk until doomsday about being surrendered Christians, but we virtually lie until we give evidence of the grace of giving in our lives. When we stand before the judgment seat of Christ to render an account of our stewardship, we will fervently regret giving so little, since it is inescapably true that what we spend we lose; what we keep will be left to others; what we give away will remain forever ours.

7

The Maintenance of the Ministry

Let him that is taught the word share in all good things with him who teaches.

Do not be deceived, God is not mocked; for whatever a man sows, that he will also reap.

For he who sows to his flesh will of the flesh reap corruption, but he who sows to the Spirit will of the Spirit reap everlasting life.

And let us not grow weary while doing good, for in due season we shall reap if we do not lose heart.

Therefore, as we have opportunity, let us do good to all, especially to those who are of the household of faith.

Galatians 6:6-10

These studies on the grace of giving would not be complete without a consideration of the maintenance of the ministry—a theme which appears again and again throughout the Bible. In Old Testament times, the priesthood was to receive "all the tithes in Israel as an inheritance in return for the work which they perform, the work of the tabernacle of meeting" (Num. 18:21). Failure of the children of Israel to keep this command was regarded as robbing God Himself; thus Jehovah's solemn words in Malachi's day, "You are cursed with

a curse, for you have robbed Me" (Mal. 3:9). In the New
Testament, the teaching concerning ministerial support is just
as strong and clear. Sending forth His disciples for their first
evangelistic crusade, the Master said, "Provide neither gold
nor silver nor copper in your moneybelts, nor bag for your
journey, nor two tunics, nor sandals, nor staffs; for a worker
is worthy of his food" (Matt. 10:9-10). In apostolic times, Paul
made it abundantly plain that "the Lord...commanded that
those who preach the gospel should live from the gospel"
(1 Cor. 9:14). Writing to Timothy, Paul reminds this young
pastor that the Scriptures teach that we should "'not muzzle
an ox while it treads out the grain,' and 'The laborer is worthy
of his wages'" (1 Tim. 5:18).

There were times, of course, when Paul—and doubtless
many of his colleagues—engaged in tentmaking and other
means of support to avoid being an expense to young churches
(1 Thess. 2:9) or giving the wrong impression to those who
were weak in the faith (1 Cor. 9:15). Generally speaking,
however, ministerial suppport was the rule of the early
churches and has continued to be so throughout the centuries.
Thus Paul provides instruction for us in Galatians 6:6-10.

It may be well to point out first that ministerial support in
most of our modern churches is on a salary basis. How this
salary is determined largely depends on the spiritual level of
the congregation. If people are instructed in the Word of God
and understand the basis on which pastors are to be paid
then all is well. On the other hand, if the policy is to hire a
man at a bargain price—irrespective of what the Scriptures
teach—then, inevitably, the church is out of favor with God
and the ministry is harmed. May God forgive those whose
outlook is embodied in the prayer of a man who rose to his
feet on one occasion and said, "Dear Lord, You keep this man
humble, and we will keep him poor."

Three matters are of immense importance in ministerial
support.

The Nature of Ministerial Support

"Let him who is taught the word share in all good things

with him who teaches." Here we have one of the clearest treatments of this matter of ministerial support anywhere in the Bible. All who profit from true evangelical preaching should pay close attention to what the Spirit of God has to say. This instruction is addressed not only to the members of a local church, but also to all who are blessed by the exposition of the Scriptures, whether it be through conference centers, crusades, over radio and television or through the printed page.

The Recognition of the Ministry of the Word

Let him who is taught the word.

It appears that even at this early date there was an organized system of teaching in the local churches that obligated believers to recognize those who were appointed and anointed to minister the truth of God. This all-important principle is sadly ignored in many of our churches today with consequent spiritual impoverishment.

Jesus was forever exhorting His disciples, "Take heed what you hear" (Mark 4:24); and again, "Take heed how you hear" (Luke 8:18). Like a refrain throughout the great hymn of His ministry, He was repeatedly saying, "He who has ears to hear, let him hear!" (Matt. 11:15; 13:9, 43). When we come to the Epistles we read statements such as these: "Let two or three prophets speak, and let the others judge"; and again: "If anyone thinks himself to be a prophet or spiritual, let him acknowledge that the things which I write to you are the commandments of the Lord" (1 Cor. 14:29, 37). Wherever there was a lack of such discernment of the true ministry of the Word Paul always lamented the fact. Think of his words to the Corinthian church, "And I, brethren, could not speak to you as to spiritual people but as to carnal, as to babes in Christ. I fed you with milk and not with solid food; for until now you were not able to receive it, and even now you are still not able" (1 Cor. 3:1-2). The writer to the Hebrews says the same thing: "For though...you ought to be teachers, you need someone to teach you again the first principles of the oracles of God; and you have come to need milk and not solid food. For everyone who partakes only of milk is unskilled in the word of righteousness, for he is a babe. But solid food belongs to those who are of full age, that is, those who by reason of use have their senses exercised to discern both good and evil" (Heb. 5:12).

So whenever there is a true recognition of the ministry of the Word there is also a corresponding responsibility not only to listen to that ministry but to support it.

The Recompense of the Ministers of the Word

Let him who is taught the word share in all good things with him who teaches.

As we have pointed out already, there was in this early period of church history an organized system of instruction in the church which demanded not only the recognition, but also the recompense of the preachers of God's truth. From the beginning the apostles warned the church, "It is not desirable that we should leave the word of God and serve tables....But [rather] we will give ourselves continually to prayer and to the ministry of the word" (Acts 6:2, 4). And so the teacher, pastor, and evangelist were dependent on the material support of those who enjoyed their ministry.

Paul is very specific in what he has to say about this matter of recompense. He says, "Let him who is taught the word share in all good things with him who teaches." The phrase "all good things" in this context means "worldly wealth." The expression is used twice in the Gospels in connection with rich people. Luke employs the expression when he relates Jesus' parable of the rich farmer who pulled down his old barns and built greater ones in order to have room to store his fruits and and his *goods* (Luke 12:18). Luke uses the same words in the story of the rich man in hell, when Abraham said to him, "Son, remember that in your lifetime you received your *good things*" (Luke 16:25; see also Rom. 15:26-27 and 1 Cor. 9:11 where carnal things are spoken of in a good sense).

The implication is clear. God never intended His servants to exist as paupers, while those who are enriched by their ministry live as princes. Only as a man is relieved from the care of providing for his own livelihood can he give adequate time to prayer, meditation, study, and his work of preaching and pastoring. Thank God all churches are not as miserly as some we know. May God have mercy on the congregations who have driven their pastors to distraction and despair because of lack of ministerial support! The British paper, *The Daily Mail,* carried the following headline a number of years ago: "The Rev. J. D. Allen, rector of Beaumont, Essex, is going to play a barrel organ to raise money for church funds." Can we imagine anything more unworthy of the high calling of a true minister of God?

The idea of poverty for the minister has been wrongly woven into Christian thought. We have been told that because Christ was born in a stable and lived as a poor man His servants should also subsist on the poverty level, but this is an altogether false argument. The greatest crime in history was the failure of men to recognize the ministry of Jesus and to recompense Him by receiving Him into their hearts and homes and giving Him of their best. Instead, it is recorded that "He came to His own [Greek, "things"], and His own did not receive Him" (John 1:11). What they did to the Master, men and women still do to preachers today! A minister has a right to expect a standard of living which is commensurate with his high and holy vocation. He has to be a leader in many areas of private and public life, and this cannot be done without compensating ministerial support. How seriously, therefore, we need to ponder this forgotten aspect of truth!

The Failure of Ministerial Support

"Do not be deceived, God is not mocked; for whatever a man sows, that he will also reap." Understood in their context, these are searching words indeed! Paul, in effect, is saying that it is most inconsistent to make large professions of love for the ministry and then to fail to support it.

Personal Deception

Do not be deceived.

Literally, this means, "Do not be led astray." A Christian's responsibility to the ministry has absolutely nothing to do with his own personal reactions to God's messenger. Truth transcends the human channel, and for the sake of truth we should support the ministry, whatever we think of "the foolishness of the message" (1 Cor. 1:21). This, of course, does not mean that we should tolerate what Paul calls "a different gospel" (Gal. 1:6), a watered-down gospel.

Some Christians were unimpressed with the preaching of the apostle Paul. They said "his bodily presence [was] weak, and his speech contemptible" (2 Cor. 10:10), and so they were led astray in fulfilling their responsibilities to this mighty man of God. We live in a day when people are sadly deceived by charisma, emotional appeals, and "persuasive words of human wisdom" (2 Cor. 2:4). Therefore, when the solid teacher of eternal truth comes along, the average listener is bored, unimpressed, and invariably fails to fulfill his solemn duty to support him.

Spiritual Rebellion

Do not be deceived, God is not mocked.

This language is deliberately used by Paul to point up an attitude of spiritual rebellion. Actually, the text reads, "Be not deceived; you cannot turn up your nose at God." No words could better describe the attitude of some people toward the content and challenge of preaching which God demands of every true minister of the Word.

A friend told me of a pastor who was taken to task by his officers. Cornering him in the vestry one Sunday morning they said, "Any more of that kind of teaching and you are out." This minister was not a liberal or even a carnal preacher; on the contrary, he was a returned missionary of great repute who had worked in the Far East for many years. He had deep fellowship with God and had an unquestionable anointing on his preaching, but members of his congregation did not want his message; so they "turned up their noses at God."

When is the great reversal going to take place? When will Christians cease to support liberal or carnal preachers who only want to fill their churches for the sake of reputation?

When are congregations going to support the word of the cross, the claims of Christ and, indeed, "the whole counsel of God" (Acts 20:27)?

Moral Corruption

Whatever a man sows, that he will also reap. For he who sows to his flesh will of the flesh reap corruption.

The surface interpretation of these words is that carnal spending will inevitably reap a carnal harvest. This is an unalterable law, and a man is a fool not to recognize it. But there is also another meaning which is inseparably linked with the apostle's general theme of ministerial support. When a congregation or an individual fails to support a spiritual ministry, in preference for a carnal ministry, the result will be loss at the judgment seat of Christ and moral corruption in the life of the church here and now. Such is the tragic story of many congregations in our land where so-called Christians are sowing to the flesh in supporting carnal ministries with resultant pollution and rottenness. May God have mercy, therefore, on individuals or groups of people who are sowing to the flesh by refusing to support the quality of preaching which God honors and blesses!

We see in unmistakable terms what Paul means by the failure of ministerial support. In the last analysis it comes right down to personal deception, spiritual rebellion, and moral corruption. Let us not be caught up in the stream of religious apostasy, lest we should be "condemned with the world" (1 Cor. 11:32).

The Pleasure of Ministerial Support

"He who sows to the Spirit will of the Spirit reap everlasting life. And let us not grow weary while doing good, for in due season we shall reap if we do not lose heart." Once again, this spiritual law lends itself to much wider application than that which Paul has in mind in this particular passage; but let us remember that Paul's primary theme is that of the maintenance of the ministry. So in a very real sense he is speaking here of the pleasure of ministerial support in a twofold way.

The Joy of Personal Stewardship

He who sows to the Spirit will of the Spirit reap everlasting life. And let us not grow weary while doing good, for in due season we shall reap if we do not lose heart.

To sow to the Spirit, in this immediate context, is to support a spiritual ministry. This support has a double reward. We add to our spiritual capital "glory, honor, and immortality" in the life to come (Rom. 2:7), and we speed the cause of the gospel to the far ends of the earth here and now. As we have seen in these studies, nothing is more worthwhile than this kind of personal stewardship. Such a ministry of support is so vital and essential to the life of the church that Paul adds, "Let us not grow weary while doing good." The verb he uses expresses physical exhaustion and relaxed effort. It describes the spiritual and moral collapse which may be caused in Christian service through lack of sustained spiritual stewardship.

My father served the Lord for thirty years in Angola, West Africa. Throughout that whole period he was never on salary. In fact, he had no guarantee from one month to another that financial support would be forthcoming. But thank God, he never lacked! He not only maintained the overhead costs of a missionary program, but he also brought up a family of three sons. In later years, when he returned home, he discovered people scattered all over the British Isles and elsewhere who had sacrificed greatly to support his work on the foreign field. In almost every case these people had been blessed by his ministry, but had chosen to remain anonymous and channel their gifts through the Echoes of Service office in Bath, England. If these people had been weary in well doing what would have happened to a lonely missionary in the heart of Africa?

The Joy of Practical Fellowship

Therefore, as we have opportunity, let us do good to all, especially to those who are of the household of faith.

That expressive phrase "the household of faith" undoubtedly includes all who are in the family of God. But in this context Paul unquestionably has in mind servants of God like himself who were dependent on personal and practical support for daily maintenance. So Paul says, "Let us do good to all, especially...those who are of the household of faith." This personal fellowship is the complement of practical support. The latter has to do with gifts and giving, while the former lays stress on deeds and doing. It is one thing to discharge our responsibility by signing a check, but quite another matter to involve ourselves in the ministry of hospitality.

Have you ever studied the subject of Christian hospitality in the New Testament? If not, you have lost out immeasurably —not only on a vital aspect of truth, but also on a most needed aspect of Christian service. Writing to the Romans, Paul follows that great passage on full surrender to the will of God with the words, "Distributing to the needs of the saints, given to hospitality" (Rom. 12:13). Instructing Timothy on the qualifications of an elder, the apostle insists that an elder must be a man "of good behavior, hospitable" (1 Tim. 3:2). Then Peter, in his exhortation to persecuted believers "in Pontus, Galatia, Cappadocia, Asia, and Bithynia" says, "Be hospitable to one another without grumbling" (1 Pet. 1:1; 4:9). But perhaps the most forceful words on this subject come from the pen of John, who commends the beloved Gaius for his hospitality and charity to traveling evangelists and preachers who had gone forth in the Savior's name, "taking nothing from the Gentiles." Concerning them John says, "We therefore ought to receive such, that we may become fellow workers for the truth" (3 John 7-8). Practical fellowship means more than financial support; it includes the cup of cold water given in the Savior's name, a meal lovingly prepared, a bed for the night, and a host of other expressions of kindness which the church of Jesus Christ so much needs. Frank Beaver pinpoints such hospitality as it pertains to pastors:

> In connection with hospitality and the often neglected expressions of kindness, we have an obligation to honor God's anointed servant. About this we have no choice. The pastor,

whoever he might be, is God's gift to the congregation. He is
not perfect, but neither is he the pastor of a perfect
church....The church is...to supply the needs of its pastor, to
be caring and loving and respectful of him."[1]

Some time ago my wife and I were graciously invited to
spend a few days with friends. We accepted the kind offer.
What overwhelmed us completely, however, was the fact that
not only was hospitality provided, along with a greatly needed
opportunity for quietness, rest, and fellowship, but also a
parting letter was handed to us which read something like
this: "Dear Friends, This is to let you know what a privilege
it has been to have you with us and to assure you of our love
and prayers." Attached to the letter was a check to cover all
our traveling expenses! I can tell you we thanked God that
such thoughtful people could be found in Christian circles
today!

Here, then, is a great subject not often handled from the
pulpit—and still less practiced in the pew; but as we have
seen it is God's truth which we cannot ignore, if we are to
be men and women of God. The Holy Spirit's ministry in this
age is to "guide [us] into all truth" (John 16:13), and we dare
not leave out any aspect of it if we mean to go all the way
with God. So let us take to heart these words of the apostle
and practice the maintenance of the ministry in our local
churches and wherever we encounter the faithful preaching
of the Word. "Let us not grow weary while doing good, for
in due season we shall reap if we do not lose heart." With
such eternal prospects in view, let me ask:

Supposing today were your last day on earth,
The last mile of the journey you've trod;
After all of your struggles, how much are you worth?
How much could you take home to God?

Don't count as possessions your silver and gold,
For tomorrow you leave them behind;

---

1. Frank Beaver, "The Pastor: Gift from God," *The Alliance Witness* 115:16 (August
6, 1980): 7-8, adapted.

And all that is yours to have and to hold
Are the blessings you've given mankind.

Just what have you done as you've journeyed along—
That was really and truly worthwhile?
Do you feel you've done good and returned it for wrong?
Could you look o'er your life with a smile?

Selected

Conclusion

Will a man rob God? Yet you have robbed Me! But you say, In what way have we robbed You? In tithes and offerings. You are cursed with a curse, for you have robbed Me, Even this whole nation. Bring all the tithes into the storehouse, that there may be food in My house, and prove Me now in this, says the Lord of hosts, if I will not open for you the windows of heaven and pour out for you such blessing that there will not be room enough to receive it.

Malachi 3:8-10

Do not lay up for yourselves treasures on earth, where moth and rust destroy and where thieves break in and steal; but lay up for yourselves treasures in heaven, where neither moth nor rust destroys and where thieves do not break in and steal. For where your treasure is, there your heart will be also.

Matthew 6:19-21

Sell what you have and give alms; provide yourselves money bags which do not grow old, a treasure in the heavens that does not fail, where no thief approaches nor moth destroys. For where your treasure is, there your heart will be also.

Luke 12:33-34

But those who desire to be rich fall into temptation and a snare, and into many foolish and harmful lusts which

91

drown men in destruction and perdition. For the love of
money is a root of all kinds of evil, for which some have
strayed from the faith in their greediness, and pierced
themselves through with many sorrows.

1 Timothy 6:9-10

Therefore by Him let us continually offer the sacrifice of
praise to God, that is, the fruit of our lips, giving thanks to
His name. But do not forget to do good and to share, for
with such sacrifices God is well pleased.

Hebrews 13:15-16

To use the words of Solomon, "Let us hear the conclusion
of the whole matter" (Eccles. 12:13). In the preceding
chapters I covered some important aspects of the grace of
giving. Now let us summarize, simply and succinctly, the areas
of truth that we have covered. I have in mind young people—
especially those who have come to me on countless occasions
asking for directives on how to motivate and manage their
ministry of giving. So I purpose to zero in on what I shall call
the dynamics and mechanics of giving.

The Dynamics of Giving

The Scripture passages that introduce this chapter contain
Paul's warning that "those who desire to be rich fall into
temptation and a snare, and into many foolish and harmful
lusts which drown men in destruction and perdition. For the
love of money is a root of all kinds of evil." In other words,
the apostle is telling us that there is something alluring and
attractive about money. Indeed, before we know it, we are
loving money! What is important, however, is that this love
of money can be either misdirected by the devil or redirected
by the Lord. This comes out in the Sermon on the Mount
where the Master declared, "Do not lay up for yourselves
treasures on earth....but lay up for yourselves treasures in
heaven....for where your treasure is, there your heart will be

also." The writer to the Hebrews reminds us, "Do not forget to do good and to share [with others, NEB], for with such sacrifices God is well pleased." These two statements contain the dynamics of giving: the love of treasure in heaven and the love of pleasure on earth. Stating these dynamics in this form will help to fix them in our minds and hearts.

Love of Treasure in Heaven

Where your treasure is, there your heart will be also.

Recall the setting of these words for a moment. Treasure or wealth among the ancients consisted in things such as clothes, gold, silver, gems, houses, lands, wine, and oil. In fact, the term defined the abundance of anything that aided the ornamentation and comforts of life. With this in view, our Lord warned, "Do not lay up for yourselves treasures on earth, where moth and rust destroy and where thieves break in and steal." Employing these figures of speech, Jesus cautions us that to set our hearts (our love) on earthly treasures will ultimately dissatisfy and even despoil us; for moths will gnaw at our clothes; rust (or, more accurately, erosion) will cause our gold, silver, and grain to vanish; and thieves will burglarize our homes. Forces in this world make the hoarding of permanent treasures here on earth impossible.

How well you and I know this! Perhaps this explains why rich people are seldom genuinely happy or secure. "Millionaires who laugh," confessed Andrew Carnegie, "are rare." Sir Ernest Cassel, a multimillionaire who spent vast fortunes for the benefit of mankind, the friend of kings and emperors, said to one of his visitors, "You may have all the money in the world and yet be a lonely and sorrowing man. The light has gone out of my life. I live in this beautiful house, which I have furnished with all the luxury and wonder of art; but, believe me, I no longer value my millions."[1]

On the other hand, our Savior advises, "Lay up for yourselves treasures in heaven....for where your treasure is, there your heart will be also." What He means is crystal clear. In the

---

1. D.M. Panton, "Laying Up Treasure," *Prairie Overcomer,* June 1964:225-228.

parallel passage in Luke 12, "the treasure in the heavens" is spelled out as the giving of alms (v. 33). This is stewardship of time, talents, and tithes in the cause of the gospel and the good of man to the glory of God. Once our hearts and minds are set on treasures in heaven, life and service become dynamic. This explains the dynamism of the early church (Acts 2:42-47) and the altruism of the apostle Paul (1 Cor. 7:30; 2 Cor. 12—15).

Dr. A. W. Tozer addressed this concept of the heavenly treasures when he wrote:

> It is one of the glories of the Christian religion that faith and love can transmute lower values into higher ones. Earthly possessions can be turned into heavenly treasures.
>
> It is like this: A twenty-dollar bill, useless in itself, can be transmuted into milk and eggs and fruit to feed hungry children. Physical and mental powers, valuable in themselves, can be transmuted into still higher values, such as a home and an education for a growing family. Human speech, a very gift of God to mankind, can become consolation for the bereaved or hope for the disconsolate, and it can rise higher and break into prayer and praise of the Most High God.
>
> As base a thing as money often is, it yet can be transmuted into everlasting treasure. It can be converted into food for the hungry and clothing for the poor; it can keep a missionary actively winning lost men to the light of the gospel and thus transmute itself into heavenly values.
>
> Any temporal possession can be turned into everlasting wealth. Whatever is given to Christ is immediately touched with immortality. Hosanna to God in the highest![2]

If our treasure is in heaven it is secure. What is more, such an investment awaits the day of rewarding dividends! The most important thing, however, is that our hearts become united instead of divided; for Jesus reminds us that "where [our] treasure is, there [our] heart will be also"; and, again, no man can "serve God and mammon [money]" (Matt. 6:24). Or, to use the language of the saintly Alexander Maclaren:

---

2. *The Alliance Witness* (October 8, 1958).

If our hearts are in heaven, then heaven will be in our hearts, and here we shall know the joy and the peace that come from "sitting in heavenly places in Christ Jesus," even whilst on earth. There is no blessedness, no stable repose, no victorious independence of the buffets and blows of life, except this, that my heart is lifted above them all, and, I was going to say, is inhaled and sucked into the life of Jesus Christ. Then if my heart is where my treasure is, and *He is my treasure,* "my life is hid with Christ in God."[3]

Love of Pleasure on Earth

Do not forget to do good and to share [what you have with others, NEB], for with such sacrifices God is well pleased (see also Phil. 4:18).

If the love of treasure in heaven is the first dynamic of giving, then the love of pleasure on earth is the second dynamic. The love of pleasure on earth, for the dedicated Christian, is the desire to please God. You will remember that this was the consuming passion of our blessed Lord. He could say, "I always do those things that please Him" (John 8:29). And Paul, recalling this, could later write, "Even Christ did not please Himself" (Rom. 15:3). No wonder the Father's voice from heaven was heard to say, "This is My beloved Son, in whom I am well pleased" (Matt. 3:17; 17:5).

If I were to ask you to state the highest ambition of your life, surely your reply would be "to please my God." And you would be right! We have learned that one of the things that brings pleasure to the heart of God is sacrificial giving, for we are told that "with such sacrifices God is well pleased." Note carefully that God is not only pleased, but well-pleased. What a dynamic motivation for life and service here on earth! Let us "honor the Lord with [our] possessions, and with the firstfruits of all [our] increase" (Prov. 3:9).

The Mechanics of Giving

If we are clear on the dynamics of giving the mechanics

---

3. Alexander Maclaren, *Expositions of Holy Scripture* [Matt. 6:24], vol. 4, (Grand Rapids: Eerdmans, 1959), p. 309.

will take care of themselves! Love always finds a way to give—regardless of circumstances or cost. But even in this matter of mechanics the Word of God is plain and practical. The grace of giving concerns four areas of our income.

The Tithes Which God Demands

Bring all the tithes into the storehouse, that there may be food in My house, and prove Me now in this, says the Lord of hosts, if I will not open for you the windows of heaven and pour out for you such blessing that there will not be room enough to receive it.

As we have noted previously in these studies, the tithe is a tenth of our income and, according to this verse in Malachi, God demands the tithe without any deductions. He declares, "Bring all the tithes." To give any less is to rob God.

Moreover, this basic principle of giving to God pervades the entire Bible. I have sought to make this clear in earlier chapters. Recall that before the law was given tithing represented the principle of giving (Gen. 14:17-24). Like the principle of the Sabbath, God introduced into the universe this rule of thumb as a guide for all ages. After the giving of the law tithing represented the precept of giving (Deut. 14:22; Neh. 10:38). With the coming of Christ tithing represented that pattern of giving. He could say, "Do not think that I came to destroy the Law or the Prophets. I did not come to destroy but to fulfill" (Matt. 5:17). It is inconceivable that our Lord would have kept every other aspect of the law and overlooked a matter such as tithing. In every area of righteous living He was—and is—our supreme example. Indeed, He referred to this matter of tithing again and again (Matt. 23:23). Even the writer to the Hebrews expressly states that tithing is a matter of fulfilling the law (Heb. 7:5). In the days of the apostles, tithing represented the privilege of giving. In his Epistle to the Romans Paul takes pains to attack what we call today "situation ethics," and he shows that no one can know the indwelling life of the Spirit without fulfilling the righteousness of the law (Rom. 8:2-4). Then he says, "love is the fulfillment of the law" (Rom. 13:10). That particular context needs to be studied, for Paul is clearly upholding the demands of the law in terms of Christian living and giving.

While Christ has taken the condemnation and curse of the law, He has in no way abrogated the outliving of the law by the power of the Spirit. In the first-century church, tithing represented the practice of giving. When Paul writes "On the first day of the week let each one of you lay something aside, storing up as [God] may prosper" (1 Cor. 16:2), he is surely referring to the biblical principle enunciated in the Scriptures. As a matter of fact, scholars have pointed out that the phrase "storing up" in that verse undoubtedly alludes to the storehouse tithing of Malachi's day. Later, in the Second Epistle of Paul to the Corinthians, Paul gives the ultimate word on this matter. He declares, "Let each one give as he purposes in his heart" (2 Cor. 9:7). The operative phrase in that text reads, "as he purposes in his heart." Such giving is not left to an unenlightened conscience or an uninstructed heart.

God never leaves us to guess when it comes to matters of faith and practice, so why should He abandon us to our own decisions and devices when it concerns one of the most important areas in the whole of human existence? We spend a great part of our lives earning money. The inescapable issue which follows concerns the management of our money, once we have acquired it. It is at this point that God breaks in with those words of prior claim, "Bring all the tithes into the storehouse."

The Offerings Which God Deserves

You have robbed Me....in tithes and offerings.

In Malachi's day the Lord had to rebuke His people for withholding the offerings as well as the tithes.

The offerings were the gifts that were brought to God, over and above the tithes. For you and me, these offerings represent our response of love for heavenly blessings. There are, for instance, the material blessings, such as an increase in salary, a successful business deal or an unexpected financial windfall. There are also spiritual blessings, such as a fresh act of surrender, a new discovery of truth, a deepened experience of God's grace or a prayerful resolve to underwrite an added responsibility in the area of stewardship. Whether blessings are material or spiritual, "Every good gift and every perfect gift is from above, and comes down from the Father of lights, with whom there is no variation or shadow of turning" (James 1:17).

When we render our tithes we look up to the throne of divine government and say, "O God, we acknowledge Thee to be the Ruler of the universe and, therefore, entitled to our tithes. We are grateful that in Thee, and in Thee alone, we live and move and have our being, Amen." When we bring our offerings, we kneel in worship before the throne of divine grace and pray, "Our Father, in response to Thy redeeming mercy, revealed in Jesus Christ, we bring the offerings of our sacrificial love and surrendered lives. Amen."

The Expenses Which God Directs

Repay no one evil for evil. Have regard for good things in the sight of all men (Rom. 12:17). Render therefore to all their due: taxes to whom taxes are due, customs to whom customs....Owe no one anything (Rom. 13:7-8).

These are pointed and practical words concerning our daily expenses. If our lives are truly yielded to God, our financial affairs will be handled with integrity and punctuality. With the directives that God has given us, we will see to it that we never live beyond our ability to meet our monetary obligations. We will avoid launching projects that cannot be underwritten with actual cash or other securities. Then, of course, we will be very careful to file our income tax returns with honesty and prompt dispatch. God says, "Render...to all their due" and this is final.

The Savings Which God Defends

The children ought not to lay up for the parents, but the parents for the children" (1 Cor. 12:14).

Paul uses another illustration from family life, declaring, "If anyone does not provide for his own, and especially for those of his household, he has denied the faith and is worse than an unbeliever [or infidel]" (1 Tim. 5:8). In my pastoral counseling, I have found tragic breakdown in this area of money matters. Husbands have failed their wives, parents have cheated their children, and grown sons and daughters have neglected their widowed mothers or other dependents. Such shortcomings are soundly and solemnly condemned by the Word of God; in fact, such dereliction of duty is described as worse than infidelity.

In light of the foregoing, it is certainly biblical and practical that savings accounts be established and insurance policies be taken out to cover the needs of dependents, emergency requirements, funeral expenses, and so on. Such financial matters should be thoroughly discussed in every Christian household. With an open Bible and in an atmosphere of prayer, our tithes, offerings, expenses, and savings should be surveyed in relation to personal, as well as general, income. Happy and healthy is the family that is united on these issues! In the last analysis, every one of us is responsible to God in time and accountable to Him in eternity (Gal. 6:2-10).

The question which usually arises at this point is whether or not these mechanics of giving actually work out in practice. The answer may appear to be simplistic and dogmatic, but it is in the affirmative, nonetheless! What God expects us to attempt He also enables us to achieve, and committed Christians have proved this to be true throughout the centuries. So let us take heart in knowing that the grace *of* giving is also the grace *for* giving.

> God made the sun—it gives.
> God made the moon—it gives.
> God made the stars—they give.
> God made the air—it gives.
> God made the clouds—they give.
> God made the earth—it gives.
> God made the sea—it gives.
> God made the trees—they give.
> God made the flowers—they give.
> God made the fowls—they give.
> God made the beasts—they give.
> God made man—he...?
>
> Selected

References

In our study of the grace of giving we have focused our attention primarily on the Corinthian letters. The subject of giving, however, has a far wider treatment in the Bible, and the Christian who desires to know "the whole counsel of God" on this important doctrine should examine carefully both Old and New Testaments. To assist such seekers after truth, the following outline and verses are prayerfully offered. It is hardly necessary to add that the material is suggestive rather than exhaustive. A good concordance, a treasury of Scripture knowledge, and a close following of cross-references will aid further research.

The Standard of Giving

Tithes

Then Melchizedek king of Salem brought out bread and wine; he was the priest of God Most High....And [Abram] gave him a tithe of all (Genesis 14:18-20).

Of all that You give me I [Jacob] will surely give a tenth to You (Genesis 28:22).

And all the tithe of the land, whether of the seed of the land or of the fruit of the tree, is the Lord's. It is holy to the Lord. If a man wants at all to redeem any of his tithes, he shall add one-fifth to it. And concerning the tithe of the herd or the flock, of whatever passes under the rod, the tenth one shall be holy to the Lord (Leviticus 27:30-32).

As soon as the commandment was circulated, the children of Israel brought in abundance the firstfruits of grain and wine, oil and honey, and of all the produce of the field; and they brought in abundantly the tithe of everything. And the children of Israel and Judah, who dwelt in the cities of Judah, brought the tithe of oxen and sheep; also the tithe of holy things which were consecrated to the Lord their God they laid in heaps (2 Chronicles 31:5-6).

To bring the firstfruits of our dough, our offerings, the fruit from all kinds of trees, the new wine and oil, to the priests, to the storerooms of the house of our God; and to bring the tithes of our land to the Levites, for the Levites should receive the tithes in all our farming communities. And the priest, the descendant of Aaron, shall be with the Levites when the Levites receive tithes; and the Levites shall bring up a tenth of the tithes to the house of our God, to the rooms of the storehouse (Nehemiah 10:37-38).

Some were appointed over the rooms of the storehouse for the offerings, the firstfruits, and the tithes, to gather into them from the fields of the cities the portions specified by the Law for the priests and Levites (Nehemiah 12:44).

And he had prepared for him a large room, where previously they had stored the grain offerings, the frankincense, the articles, the tithes of grain, the new wine and oil, which were commanded to be given to the Levites and singers and gatekeepers, and the offerings for the priests....Then all Judah brought the tithe of the grain and the new wine and the oil to the storehouse (Nehemiah 13:5, 12).

Honor the Lord with your possessions, and with the firstfruits of all your increase (Proverbs 3:9).

The ephah and the bath shall be of the same measure, so that the bath contains one-tenth of a homer, and the ephah one-tenth of a homer; their measure shall be according to the homer (Ezekiel 45:11.)

Bring your sacrifices every morning, your tithes every three days (Amos 4:4).

Will a man rob God? Yet you have robbed Me! But you say, In what way have we robbed You? In tithes and offerings. You are cursed with a curse, for you have robbed Me, even this whole nation. Bring all the tithes into the storehouse, that there may be food in My house, and prove Me now in this, says the Lord of hosts (Malachi 3:8-10).

Woe to you, scribes and Pharisees, hypocrites! For you pay tithe of mint and anise and cumin, and have neglected the weightier matters of the law: justice and mercy and faith. These you ought to have done, without leaving the others undone (Matthew 23:23).

But woe to you Pharisees! For you tithe mint and rue and all manner of herbs, and pass by justice and the love of God. These you ought to have done, without leaving the others undone. (Luke 11:42).

I fast twice a week; I give tithes of all that I possess (Luke 18:12).

(see also Numbers 18:21-32; Deuteronomy 12:5-19; 14:22-29; 26:12-15; Hebrews 7:2, 4, 8-9).

Offerings

Everyone included among those who are numbered, from twenty years old and above, shall give an offering to the Lord. The rich shall not give more and the poor shall not give less than half a shekel, when you give an offering to the Lord, to make atonement for yourselves (Exodus 30:14-15).

And all the gold of the offering that they offered to the Lord, from the captains of thousands and captains of hundreds, was sixteen thousand seven hundred and fifty shekels (Numbers 31:52).

And all those who were around them encouraged them with articles of silver and gold, with goods and livestock, and with precious things, besides all that was willingly offered (Ezra 1:6).

Some of the heads of the fathers' houses, when they came

to the house of the Lord which is in Jerusalem, offered freely for the house of God, to erect it in its place (Ezra 2:68).

And afterward they offered the regular burnt offering, and those for New Moons and for all the appointed feasts of the Lord that were consecrated, and those of everyone who willingly offered a freewill offering to the Lord (Ezra 3:5).

All the silver and gold that you may find in all the province of Babylon, along with the freewill offering of the people and the priests, are to be freely offered for the house of their God in Jerusalem (Ezra 7:16).

And [Eliashib the priest] had prepared for [Tobiah] a large room, where previously they had stored the grain offerings, the frankincense, the articles, the tithes of grain, the new wine and oil, which were commanded to be given to the Levites and singers and gatekeeper, and the offerings for the priests (Nehemiah 13:5).

Will a man rob God? Yet you have robbed Me! But you say, In what way have we robbed You? In tithes and offerings (Malachi 3:8).

Every priest taken from among men is appointed for men in things pertaining to God, that he may offer both gifts and sacrifices for sins....He is required...to offer for sins (Hebrews 5:1, 3).

There are priests who offer...gifts according to the law (Hebrews 8:4).

(see also Exodus 35:4-29; 1 Chronicles 29:6-17; 2 Chronicles 31:10-14; Nehemiah 10:37-39).

Sacrifices

I have all and abound. I am full, having received from Epaphroditus the things which were sent from you, a sweet-smelling aroma, an acceptable sacrifice, well-pleasing to God (Philippians 4:18).

By Him let us continually offer the sacrifice of praise to God, that is, the fruit of our lips, giving thanks to His name....do not forget to do good and to share, for with such sacrifices God is well pleased (Hebrews 13:15-16).

Collections

The king called Jehoiada the chief priest, and said to him, Why have you not required the Levites to bring in from Judah and from Jerusalem the collection, according to the commandment of Moses...for the tabernacle of witness? (2 Chronicles 24:6).

Then the disciples, each according to his ability, determined to send relief to the brethren...in Judea (Acts 11:29, relief).

It pleased those from Macedonia and Achaia to make a certain contribution for the poor among the saints...in Jerusalem (Romans 15:26, contribution).

Now concerning the collection for the saints... (1 Corinthians 16:1).

The Substance of Giving

Increase

When you have finished laying aside all the tithe of your increase in the third year, which is the year of tithing....then you shall say before the Lord your God...I have removed the holy tithe from my house, and also have given them to the Levite, the stranger, the fatherless, and the widow, according to all Your commandments which You have commanded me; I have not transgressed Your commandments, nor have I forgotten them (Deuteronomy 26:12, 13).

Honor the Lord with your possessions, and with the firstfruits of all your increase (Proverbs 3:9).

(see also Deuteronomy 14:22-28).

Riches

Wealth and riches will be in his house, and his righteousness endures forever (Psalm 112:3).

God has given riches and wealth, and given [every man] power to eat of it, to receive his heritage and rejoice in his labor—this is the gift of God (Ecclesiastes 5:19).

Let not the wise man glory in his wisdom, let not the mighty man glory in his might, nor let the rich man glory in his riches; but let him who glories glory in this, that he understands and knows Me...the Lord (Jeremiah 9:23-24).

We make known to you the grace of God bestowed on the churches of Macedonia; that in a great trial of affliction the abundance of their joy and their deep poverty abounded in the riches of their liberality (2 Corinthians 8:1-2).

Worthy is the Lamb who was slain to receive power and riches and wisdom, and strength and honor and glory and blessing (Revelation 5:12)!

(see also 1 Chronicles 29).

Treasures

In this trusted office were four chief gatekeepers; they were Levites. And they had charge over the chambers and treasuries of the house of God (1 Chronicles 9:26).

Then David gave his son Solomon the plans for....the treasuries of the house of God, and of the treasuries for the dedicated things (1 Chronicles 28:11, 12).

Hezekiah had very great riches and honor. And he made himself treasuries for silver, for gold, for precious stones, for spices, for shields, and for all kinds of desirable items (2 Chronicles 32:27).

Then all Judah brought the tithe of the grain and the new wine and the oil to the storehouse. And I appointed... treasurers over the storehouse....and their task was to distribute to their brethren (Nehemiah 13:12, 13).

In the house of the righteous there is much treasure (Proverbs 15:6).

Do not lay up for yourselves treasures on earth, where moth and rust destroy and where thieves break in and steal; but lay up for yourselves treasures in heaven, where neither moth nor rust destroys and where thieves do not break in and steal. For where your treasure is, there your heart will be also (Matthew 6:19-21).

Jesus said to him, If you want to be perfect, go, sell what

you have and give to the poor, and you will have treasure in heaven; and come, follow Me (Matthew 19:21).

Then Jesus [looked at the rich young ruler], and said to him, One thing you lack: Go your way, sell whatever you have and give to the poor, and you will have treasure in heaven; and come, take up the cross, and follow Me (Mark 10:21).

Now Jesus sat opposite the treasury and saw how the people put money into the treasury....Then one poor widow came and threw in two mites....So He called His disciples to Him and said to them, Assuredly,...this poor widow has put in more than all those who have given to the treasury (Mark 12:41-43).

Sell what you have and give alms; provide...a treasure in the heavens that does not fail, where no thief approaches nor moth destroys. For where your treasure is, there your heart will be also (Luke 12:33-34).

These words Jesus spoke in the treasury, as He taught in the temple; and no one laid hands on Him, for His hour had not yet come (John 8:20).

(see also Joshua 6:19-24; Nehemiah 7:68-72).

Good(s)

Jesus said, Let her alone. Why do you trouble her? She has done a good work for Me (Mark 14:6).

If you then, being evil, know how to give good gifts to your children, how much more will your heavenly Father give the Holy Spirit to those who ask Him (Luke 11:13)!

But Abraham said, Son, remember that in your lifetime you received your good things, and likewise Lazarus evil things; but now he is comforted and you are tormented (Luke 16:25).

At Joppa there was a certain disciple named...Dorcas. This woman was full of good works and charitable deeds which she did (Acts 9:36).

Let us consider one another in order to stir up love and good works (Hebrews 10:24).

Do not forget to do good and to share, for with such sacrifices God is well pleased (Hebrews 13:16).

As each one has received a gift, minister it to one another, as good stewards of the manifold grace of God (1 Peter 4:10).

But whoever has this world's goods, and sees his brother in need, and shuts up his heart from him, how does the love of God abide in him? (1 John 3:17).

(see also Deuteronomy 6:6-25; Galatians 6:6-10).

Gifts

So it shall be on Aaron's forehead, that Aaron may bear the iniquity of the holy things which the children of Israel hallow in all their holy gifts; and it shall always be on his forehead, that they may be accepted before the Lord (Exodus 28:38).

The kings of Tarshish and of the isles will bring presents; the kings of Sheba and Seba will offer gifts (Psalm 72:10).

Many entreat the favor of the nobility, and every man is a friend to one who gives gifts (Proverbs 19:6).

And when they had come into the house, they saw the young Child with Mary His mother, and fell down and worshiped Him. And when they had opened their treasures, they presented gifts to Him: gold, frankincense, and myrrh (Matthew 2:11).

Therefore if you bring your gift to the altar, and there remember that your brother has something against you, leave your gift there before the altar, and go your way. First be reconciled to your brother, and then come and offer your gift (Matthew 5:23-24).

And Jesus said to him, See that you tell no one; but go your way, show yourself to the priest, and offer the gift that Moses commanded, as a testimony to them (Matthew 8:4).

And whoever swears by the altar, it is nothing; but whoever swears by the gift that is on it, he is obliged to perform it. Fools and blind! For which is greater, the gift or the altar that sanctifies the gift? (Matthew 23:18-19).

Not that I seek the gift, but I seek the fruit that abounds to your account (Philippians 4:17).

For every priest taken from among men is appointed for men in things pertaining to God, that he may offer both gifts and sacrifices for sins (Hebrews 5:1).

Every high priest is appointed to offer both gifts and sacrifices. Therefore it is necessary that this One also have something to offer. For if He were on earth, He would not be a priest, since there are priests who offer the gifts according to the law (Hebrews 8:3-4).

The way into the Holiest of All was not yet made manifest while the first tabernacle was still standing. It was symbolic for the present time in which both gifts and sacrifices are offered which cannot make him who performed the service perfect in regard to the conscience (Hebrews 9:8-9).

(see also Numbers 18:6-29).

Money

And you shall take the atonement money of the children of Israel, and shall appoint it for the service of the tabernacle of meeting, that it may be a memorial for the children of Israel before the Lord, to make atonement for yourselves (Exodus 30:16).

They also gave money to the masons and the carpenters, and food, drink, and oil to the people of Sidon and Tyre to bring cedar logs from Lebanon to the sea at Joppa, according to the permission which they had from Cyrus king of Persia (Ezra 3:7).

Show Me the tax money. So they brought Him a denarius (Matthew 22:19).

But he who had received one [talent] went and dug in the ground, and hid his lord's money....His lord answered and said to him, You wicked and lazy servant,....you ought to have deposited my money with the bankers, and at my coming I would have received back my own with interest (Matthew 25:18, 26, 27).

Jesus sat opposite the treasury and saw how the people

put money into the treasury (Mark 12:41).

And Joses, who was also named Barnabas by the apostles
...having land, sold it, and brought the money and laid it at
the apostles' feet (Acts 4:37).

(see also 2 Chronicles 24:5-14; 34:9-14; Luke 19:12-27).

Possessions

When the young man heard that saying, he went away
sorrowful, for he had great possessions (Matthew 19:22).

All who believed were together and had all things in
common, and sold their possessions and goods, and divided
them among all, as anyone had need (Acts 2:45).

Nor was there anyone among them who lacked; for all who
were possessors of lands or houses sold them, and brought
the proceeds of the things that were sold (Acts 4:34).

But a certain man named Ananias, with Sapphira his wife,
sold a possession (Acts 5:1).

Wealth

You say in your heart, My power and the might of my hand
have gained me this wealth. [But] you shall remember the
Lord your God, for it is He who gives you power to get wealth
(Deuteronomy 8:17-18).

And Naomi had a kinsman of her husband's, a man of great
wealth...; his name was Boaz (Ruth 2:1).

And God said to Solomon: Because this was in your heart,
and you have not asked riches or wealth or honor or the life
of your enemies, nor have you asked long life—but have asked
wisdom and knowledge for yourself, that you may judge My
people over whom I have made you king—wisdom and
knowledge are granted to you; and I will give you riches and
wealth and honor, such as none of the kings have had who
have been before you, nor shall any after you have the like
(2 Chronicles 1:11-12).

Wealth and riches will be in his house, and his righteousness
endures forever (Psalm 112:3).

The rich man's wealth is his strong city; the destruction of the poor is their poverty (Proverbs 10:15).

Wealth makes many friends, but the poor is separated from his friend (Proverbs 19:4).

As for every man to whom God has given riches and wealth, and given him power to eat of it, to receive his heritage and rejoice in his labor — this is the gift of God (Ecclesiastes 5:19).

The Spirit of Giving

Liberality

Moreover, brethren, we make known to you the grace of God bestowed on the churches of Macedonia: that in a great trial of affliction the abundance of their joy and their deep poverty abounded in the riches of their liberality (2 Corinthians 8:1-2).

Through the proof of this ministry they glorify God for the obedience of your confession to the gospel of Christ, and for your liberal sharing with them and all men (2 Corinthians 9:13).

(see also Deuteronomy 15:12-15; Proverbs 11:24-26).

Charity (Love)

Jesus said to him, You shall love the Lord your God with all your heart, with all your soul, and with all your mind. This is the first and great commandment. And the second is like it: You shall love your neighbor as yourself (Matthew 22:37-39).

And though I bestow all my goods to feed the poor, and though I give my body to be burned, but have not love, it profits me nothing (1 Corinthians 13:3).

But as you abound in everything — in faith, in speech, in knowledge, in all diligence, and in your love for us — see that you abound in this grace also. I speak not by commandment, but I am testing the sincerity of your love by the diligence of others....Therefore show to them, and before the churches, the proof of your love and of our boasting on your behalf

(2 Corinthians 8:7-8, 24, love).

We give thanks to God always for you....remembering without ceasing your work of faith, labor of love, and patience of hope in our Lord Jesus Christ in the sight of our God and Father (1 Thessalonians 1:2, 3).

Timothy has come to us from you, and brought us good news of your faith and love,...that you always have good remembrance of us, greatly desiring to see us, as we also to see you (1 Thessalonians 3:6).

For God is not unjust to forget your work and labor of love which you have shown toward His name, in that you have ministered to the saints, and do minister (Hebrews 6:10).

Let us consider one another in order to stir up love and good works (Hebrews 10:24).

By this we know love, because He laid down His life for us. And we also ought to lay down our lives for the brethren. But whoever has this world's goods, and sees his brother in need, and shuts up his heart from him, how does the love of God abide in him? (1 John 3:16-17).

The brethren and...strangers....have borne witness of your love before the church. If you send them forward on their journey in a manner worthy of God, you will do well (3 John 5,6).

I know your works, love, service, faith, and your patience; and as for your works, the last are more than the first (Revelation 2:19).

Hilarity

In a great trial of affliction the abundance of their joy and their deep poverty abounded in the riches of their liberality (2 Corinthians 8:2, joy).

So let each one give as he purposes in his heart, not grudgingly or of necessity; for God loves a cheerful giver (2 Corinthians 9:7, cheerfulness).

(see also Ezra 6:15-18).

Hospitality

Distributing to the needs of the saints, given to hospitality (Romans 12:13).

A bishop then must be blameless, the husband of one wife, temperate, sober-minded, of good behavior, hospitable, able to teach (1 Timothy 3:2).

A bishop must be blameless....hospitable, a lover of what is good, sober-minded, just, holy, self-controlled (Titus 1:7,8).

Let brotherly love continue. Do not forget to entertain strangers, for by so doing some have unwittingly entertained angels (Hebrews 13:1-2).

Be hospitable to one another without grumbling (1 Peter 4:9).

The Secret of Giving

Giving

Speak to the children of Israel, and say to them: When you come into the land which I give to you, and reap its harvest, then you shall bring a sheaf of the firstfruits of your harvest to the priest (Leviticus 23:10; see also v. 38).

He administers justice for the fatherless and the widow, and loves the stranger, giving him food and clothing (Deuteronomy 10:18).

The kings of Tarshish and of the isles will bring presents; the kings of Sheba and Seba will offer gifts. Yes, all kings shall fall down before Him; all nations shall serve Him (Psalm 72:10-11).

Freely you have received, freely give (Matthew 10:8).

Give alms of such things as you have (Luke 11:41).

I have shown you in every way, by laboring like this, that you must support the weak. And remember the words of the Lord Jesus, that He said, It is more blessed to give than to receive (Acts 20:35).

(see also Exodus 30:12-15).

Scattering

There is one who scatters, yet increases more; and there is one who withholds more than is right, but it leads to poverty (Proverbs 11:24).

Sowing

He who sows sparingly will also reap sparingly, and he who sows bountifully will also reap bountifully....May He who supplies seed to the sower, and bread for food, supply and multiply the seed you have sown and increase the fruits of your righteousness (2 Corinthians 9:6, 10).

Do not be deceived, God is not mocked; for whatever a man sows, that he will also reap. For he who sows to his flesh will of the flesh reap corruption, but he who sows to the Spirit will of the Spirit reap everlasting life (Galatians 6:7-8).

Communicating/Sharing

For I bear witness that according to their ability, yes and beyond their ability, they were freely willing, imploring us with much urgency that we would receive the gift and the fellowship of the ministering to the saints (2 Corinthians 8:3-4).

And I went up by revelation, and communicated to them that gospel which I preach among the Gentiles, but privately to those who were of reputation, lest by any means I might run, or had run, in vain (Galatians 2:2).

Let him who is taught the word share in all good things with him who teaches (Galatians 6:6, showing fellowship).

I thank my God....for your fellowship in the gospel from the first day until now (Philippians 1:3, 5).

Nevertheless you have done well that you shared in my distress. Now you Philippians know also that in the beginning of the gospel, when I departed from Macedonia, no church shared with me concerning giving and receiving but you only (Philippians 4:14-15).

Let them do good, that they be rich in good works, ready to give, willing to share (1 Timothy 6:18).

I thank my God, making mention of you always in my prayers....that the sharing of your faith may become effective by the acknowledgment of every good thing which is in you in Christ Jesus (Philemon 1:4, 6).

But do not forget to do good and to share, for with such sacrifices God is well pleased (Hebrews 13:16).

We therefore ought to receive [the brethren and...strangers], that we may become fellow workers for the truth (3 John 8).

The System of Giving

The Where of Giving

Now concerning the collection for the saints,...I have given orders to the churches (1 Corinthians 16:1).

The When of Giving

On the first day of the week (1 Corinthians 16:2).

The Who of Giving

Let each one of you (1 Corinthians 16:2).

The What of Giving

Let each one of you lay something aside, storing up as [God] may prosper....Let each one give as he purposes in his heart, not grudgingly or of necessity (1 Corinthians 16:2; 2 Corinthians 9:7).

The Why of Giving

God loves a cheerful giver (2 Corinthians 9:7).

The Service of Giving

Giving Supports the Weak of the Church

Now all who believed were together, and had all things in common, and sold their possessions and goods, and divided them among all, as anyone had need. So continuing daily with one accord in the temple, and breaking bread from house to house, they ate their food with gladness and simplicity of heart, praising God and having favor with all the people. And the Lord added to the church daily those who were being saved (Acts 2:44-47).

I have shown you in every way, by laboring like this, that you must support the weak. And remember the words of the Lord Jesus, that He said, It is more blessed to give than to receive (Acts 20:35).

(see also Acts 4:32-37; 2 Corinthians 8:1-24; 9:1-15).

Giving Sustains the Work of the Church

I thank my God upon every remembrance of you,....for your fellowship in the gospel from the first day until now (Philippians 1:3, 5).

Nevertheless you have done well that you shared in my distress. Now you Philippians know also that in the beginning of the gospel, when I departed from Macedonia, no church shared with me concerning giving and receiving but you only (Philippians 4:14-15).

For God is not unjust to forget your work and labor of love which you have shown toward His name, in that you have ministered to the saints, and do minister (Hebrews 6:10).

(see also 1 Corinthians 9:9-14; Galatians 6:6-10).

A critical examination of the foregoing references will reveal that in many instances *one* English word is employed to express a variety of Hebrew or Greek terms in the Old or New Testaments respectively. For example, the word in the original texts translated *tithe* or *tithing* may have different shades of meaning not apparent in our English translations. This fact, however, only serves to enrich and enforce the doctrine of the grace of giving. Continue to read, learn, mark, and inwardly digest what God has to say on this subject until knowledge becomes action.

Additional Reading

Alcorn, Randy. *Your Money and Posessions: Making Them Count for Eternity.* Wheaton: Ill.: Tyndale, 1989.

Baldwin, Stanley G. *Your Money Matters.* Minneapolis: Bethany, 1977.

Blue, Ron. *Master Your Money: A Step by Step Plan for Financial Freedom.* Nashville: Nelson, 1986.

Bruso, Dick. *Bible Promises: Help & Hope for Your Finances.* San Bernardino, Calif.: Here's Life, 1985.

Burkett, Larry. *What the Bible Says About Money.* Brentwood, Tenn.: Wolgemuth & Hyatt, 1989.

Clark, Henry B. *Escape from the Money Trap.* Judson, 1973.

Clinard, Turner N. *Responding to God: The Life of Stewardship.* Philadelphia: Westminster, 1980.

Cunningham, Richard B. *Creative Stewardship.* Nashville: Abingdon, 1979.

Dayton, Howard L., Jr. *Your Money: Frustration or Freedom?* Wheaton, Ill.: Tyndale, 1979.

Deitz, Charles E. *God's Trustees.* St. Louis: Bethany, 1976.

Fisher, Wallace E. *All the Good Gifts: On Doing Bible Stewardship.* Minneapolis: Augsburg, 1979.

Fooshee, Jr., George. *You Can Be Financially Free.* Old Tappan, N.J.: Revell, 1976.

Foster, Richard. *The Challenge of the Disciplined Life (formerly Money, Sex and Power).* San Francisco: Harper & Row, 1985.

Getz, Gene A. *A Biblical Theology of Material Possessions.* Chicago: Moody Press, 1990.

117

Hales, Edward J. and Alan J. Youngren. *Your Money, Their Ministry: A Guide to Responsible Christian Giving.* Grand Rapids: Eerdmans, 1981.

Hancock, Maxine. *Living on Less and Liking It More.* Eugene, Oreg.: Harvest House, 1984.

Hobbs, Herschel. *The Epistles to the Corinthians.* Grand Rapids: Baker, 1960.

Kendall R. T., *Tithing: A Call to Serious, Biblical Giving.* Grand Rapids: Zondervan, 1983.

Knudsen, Raymond B. *Developing Dynamic Stewardship.* Nashville: Abingdon, 1978.

Laidlaw, Robert A. *Giving to God*, 3rd ed. London: Living Waters Missionary Union.

MacArthur, Jr., John. *Giving God's Way.* Wheaton, Ill.: Tyndale House Publishers, 1988.

McGinty, John. *How to Raise the Level of Giving in Your Church.* St. Louis: Bethany, 1979.

Murray, Andrew. *Christ's Perspective on the Use and Abuse of Money.* Minneapolis: Bethany, 1978.

Rees, Tom. *Money Talks.* Otford Hills, Sevenoaks, Kent, England: Hildenborough Hall.

Salstrand, George A. E. *The Grace of Giving.* Grand Rapids: Baker, 1964.

_____. *A Good Steward.* Grand Rapids: Baker, 1965.

_____. *The Tithe: The Minimum Standard for Christian Giving.* Grand Rapids: Baker, 1952.

Shedd, Charlie W. *How to Develop a Tithing Church.* Nashville: Abingdon, 1961.

Watts, Wayne. *The Gift of Giving.* Colorado Springs: NavPress 1982.

Webley, Simon. *How to Give Away Your Money.* Madison: InterVarsity. 1979.

Willmer, Wesley K., ed. *Money For Ministries.* Wheaton, Ill.: Scripture Press, 1989.

Other Books by Stephen F. Olford

Books

Heart-Cry for Revival
Preaching the Word of God
The Tabernacle: Camping with God

Booklets

Becoming a Child of God
Becoming a Man of God
Becoming a Servant of God
Encounter with Anxiety
Encounter with Fear
Encounter with Loneliness
Manna in the Morning

Institute for Biblical Preaching

(Expository resources, vols. 1-7)